Eldon Grier:
Collected Poems
1955-2000

BOOKS OF POETRY:

A Morning From Scraps (1955) Majorca, Spain
Poems (1956)
The Ring of Ice (1957) Cambridge Press
Manzanillo And Other Poems (1958)
A Friction of Lights (1963)   Contact Press
Pictures On The Skin (1967) Delta Press
Selected Poems, 1955-1970 (1971) Delta Press
The Assassination of Colour (1978) Fiddlehead
Collected Poems, 1955-2000 (2000, Ekstasis Editions)

RADIO PLAYS:

"Fitzgerald and my Father," CBC Radio, Don Mowatt, Producer
"Monet at Giverney," CBC Radio, Don Mowatt, Producer

COLLECTED
POEMS
1955-2000

ELDON GRIER

Ekstasis  Editions

Canadian Cataloguing in Publication Data

Grier, Eldon, 1917-
        Collected Poems

        Poems
        ISBN 1-896860-82-6

        I. Title.
        PS8513.R58A17 2001   C811'.54   C00-911395-9
        PR9199.3.G763A17 2001

© Eldon Grier, 2001.
Cover : Drawing by the author   design/photo by Sylvia Tait

Acknowledgements:
Thanks to all past publishers, and small mags who have published my poems over the years, Louis Dudek, Ralph Gustafson, who first anthologized this fledgling poet, John Robert Columbo, Contact Press, Delta Canada, Fiddlehead, Cambridge Press, Ekstasis Editions, The League of Canadian Poets, The C.B.C., Don Mowatt, The Canada Council for the Arts, B.C. Cultural Services. Special thanks to John Ivor Smith for his computer skills and generosity in relation to this book, and to my friends and family for their continued support, and to my wife, Sylvia. And to all the wonderful artists of the world, past and present, who have inspired me to write.

Published in 2001 by:
Ekstasis Editions Canada Ltd.   Ekstasis Editions
Box 8474, Main Postal Outlet   Box 571
Victoria, B.C. V8W 3S1   Banff, Alberta T0L 0C0

THE CANADA COUNCIL | LE CONSEIL DES ARTS
FOR THE ARTS | DU CANADA
SINCE 1957 | DEPUIS 1957

Collected Poems, 1955-2001 has been published with the assistance of a grant from the Canada Council and the Cultural Services Branch of British Columbia.

Dedicated in loving memory for my son, Brock Eldon Grier.

CONTENTS

Section One

We Drive The River Road From Quebec

We drive the river road from Quebec straight
Into the rolling eye of the sun
Its warmth is a wine that loosens my thighs.
Robert has his head on Madeline's lap,
And John watches the way, lazy as a cat.

We have picnicked on the Champs de Bataille
With long stick loaves of bread,
Vin rouge and cheese. The taste of
The sun was our dessert, and the river
Curved gravely below us like the Milky Way.

We drive the river road from Quebec, suspended
In our speeding sling of ease.
Fragile clock flowers interpolate the facts
As we touch the great coils of the river
Like sleepers passing in a dream.

The first clear day of a cold spring brings
six of us to Quebec

in high spirits.

The terrain is as sensational to us as it
was to the generals.

We find beauty shorn of doubtful motives.

QUEBEC

At steeplecock height
In a tousling wind,
Bands of tourists,
Ants in the spiral
Dimension of birds,
Stalk the pale
Ghosts of history.
Bet on each parroting guide
For signs of the dead.
But brother, nobody's home
Except the river
With its carnival of ships
And the dizzying miles.
Forget your books and cameras.
Dream you flew here
And that lunchtime never comes.
History is in the hotel lounges;
The delicate Wolfe,
Dying in a bed of flags,
Or Montcalm, propped in the backstage
Ruin of battle.

November 1956

There are the refineries,
　　　The river in a final curve,
There is the city in its hard grey shell
　　　　　humming complacently.

Here is the lookout, the pigeons landing,
Blowing with spume;
　　　　　the iron cross
Criss-crossed, wounding the air:
the steps
The pampered wood.
The fallen oak leaves
　　　　　half submerged
Dotting the snow with jagged fins.

There is the sun
　　　　glazing the land
The pencil of the university.
　　　The cemetery hill
　　　　　which seems to be caught
In a dark rain.

There against the landlocked west
　　　The chutes and black retorts
Of the coke-ovens,
The agile spurs of smoke
　　　　　dissolving as they grow.

Here the farm of Christian Smith
Who died a hundred years ago
　　　　　escaping the pox.

Here a poet
　　　hunching in the wind.
Intentionally trapped like McClure
　　　　　in a ring of ice.

HOLIDAY

Every holiday brings a sprawl of people
Nestling the close pockets of the park,
Wrestling the day's disorder
With something like humour.

Find the finely polished Venus
In the mother expecting nothing more.
And how conceivably
Came the resonant Commandments
From a tooth-fringed hyena hole?

Metamorphosis

Converting a comptometer operator
Into a clown's assistant
Isn't easy.

But take the case of Florence,
Irish Florence,
Whose eyes are blue
As sky by Poussin,
As some old and forgotten blue
That was blue for everyone.
Was it lapis lazuli?

For Watteau she was Pierrot's sister.
And for Renoir, she posed in tights
With an orange in her hand.

ARTIST BEWARE

O artist beware
The saintly family life,
The Sunday of destruction,
And the insect death.

Pursue the wondrous
Innermost of art. Watch for it
At the corner of the night,
And in the sudden intuition
Of morning, nor mistake
The chameleon horror
Of the dream.

And people, receive him gently,
For here is stillness and majesty
For a crumble of convict guilt.

LAFONTAINE PARK

As I do not expect
The strong new world or kingdom come,
I await with confident expectation
A fusion of images.

Strolling in Lafontaine Park with Sharon
(The fragrance of children does not need the poet)
We record the readymade bear
And a goat as linear as Leonardo.
And the perpetual excitement of the pheasants
Leads to the colour of turtle-dove.

Honk! Honk!

Both of us laugh.
What an absurd bird
Skeltering about the cage
In a frenetic rage,
Snapping the steady graph of perception
Triggering the dark drop.

My Father and his brother Harold,
You should have known them,
Left no works only legend.
Both were religious men,
Unscientific Hedonists, irresistibly
Swaying all but the very weak,
Expending life like colour,
And meeting the grotesque heresy of death
With churlish disbelief
Their formless gift lavished
On the narrow range of aquaintance
Haunts me with its imperfection.

Living is determined
Not so much by environment
As a never to be resolved pattern of conflict
Down the generations.

My Father's Father was a lumber merchant.
His works were many.
Come and see his roll top desk
And the nail to hang his pocket watch.
There goes his name on a truck.
He did not wish to live in the hearts of men,
But his careful accounting
May outlast his childrens' children.

And so here am I,
A third permutation
Or the thirty-third,
Not wishing to conserve or to spend
But rather to transform.
And now
There is the little girl, Sharon.

Who would have thought the day
Would have been so full of May
So heavily scented.
Only the water in the serpentine
Is stagnant with a summer slime.
Below us the canoes
In italianate hues
Are stretched out on the quay
Like mammals flopped up from the sea,
The red nuzzling the green.
And in the dreamy measure
Of a landscape ordered up for pleasure,
Nothing can come of serious intent,
Nothing could be really seriously meant.
The old man waggling his finger
At his lounging friends
Might be believed two streets away.

And by the way,
The tired droning sound
Coming from the ultimate suspension
Of the peaceful sky—
Sharon doesn't even hear it,
Has lost its menace
Dropping to the ground,
Sounds like beneficent invention
To a people
Made drowsy with contradiction.
"Oh my Papa, to me you were so wonderful." "*Prends garde,
ma petite, tu va tomber.*" Strolling in the park with Sharon,
Doing the backward multiplication
Of conception—
Awaiting the new words.

Five Bronze Figures From The Congo (Contemporary)

At six inches high
The figures swing past below a window
Or beneath a heavy jungle branch;
The thin rough shafts and arrowheads
Of their physiques molten with alertness.
They could be Negroes
Masquerading as Greeks, or Greeks in
A rare black moment of spontaneous fun,
Or pagan actors parading into town; the drum,
The short striped coat, the helmet, and the rest.
But what really makes them unique
Is a musical kind of ease; a
Limpidness of form as irresistible to the mind
As five quick notes of a flute.

Ice-Breaker

Someone built it
With an eye for theatre;
The bunched ellipses,
And the tripod
Mast as foil, its
Proletarian purpose
Dramatized by this
Particular powerful look.

Backing, stopping,
Shooting squid ink in
The air, it comes
To life with a dozen
Different implications,
Charges in the ice
With a kind of
Concentrated masculinity.

But this is no
Carnival dragon, no
Demolition machine in
A euphemistic shell.
Crushing crudely,
Racy with a
Country captain's touch,
It does less
Than keep a river running,
More than cut the
First grey leaves
Into the spring torrent.

For Mervin

Before, all in black
You would have sat in the sun,
One of the privileged ones
Debating
Learning to affirm the old principles.

Tall in the manner of young Americans,
Benign, ruddy-complexioned,
You now converge (you must)
On the habit of generations,
Quit the job you so skillfully filled
To search back through time-landscapes,
Through Rome
Bright and thin this autumn as
A newly cleaned masterpiece.

What you will find (your selection)
Is so far undefined,
A new version of the David Star
Softer perhaps around the edges
But still hieratic,
Starfish-centred,
And spiked with cardinals points.

THROUGH THE STRANGE SWEET MARRIAGE OF MY UNCLE

through the strange sweet marriage

of an uncle we

took to visiting Long Island

had lunch with Rachmaninoff

at the age of five

saw "twenties" movie happening

scaffolding out on the lawn

actors hooked on some zany

early eating routines...

at Briarcliff Manor

later a school for girls later still

a sanctuary for the anxious

I was anxious once

beating my water wings

into a pair of faceless tanks

like all New York the pool

forgot to shout   lay pure about me

like a magician's handkerchief...

perhaps I'd be

described as nobody boy   my uncle's

thing was humour   great but

fatal as a vice   my parents

had the stunningest credentials

everything royal except the mind

everything exposed   my cousin

adorable as child became

for me replaced

a California lesbian

as the cosmopolitan Russian

played piano *en famille*

my uncle let his crow loose

he had to it seems   I hope this leaked

a scratch on all the steaming wealth

Goya on the stairs

Rembrandt captive in the library...

dreamy animal children lost

to strict accountancy

sullen bankers with pustular noses

bankers with

salmon streams in Canada

movie magic out on their lawns

stake in the treacherous prize of America

in wheeling steely America Sun

GREAT TIMES

Those were great times
When my father would decide to take
Us out on the town.
One night, I remember, we started with doubles
And by the time we reached the hotel
All tastes had become one.

We were still together
At the Russian place
          (The doorman wears an astrakhan).
"Where you bin?" he asked.
"We bin dead," we said.

Then the fat headwaiter
Advancing on us like a great
Pimp of pleasure and
The tall bottles stacking up in the middle
Of the table,
Pulse became the beat of the band and
The red walls, the red roaring in our heads.
          And how we smiled—
                    great neon smiles
Looping us around the table.

"These your boys Chas?"

How we smiled
                    until the room
Became the brown sea roaring, and mermaids laughed
Below the seventh level of the sea.

GRANDFATHER BLACK

a size that's hard
to compress grandfather
Irishman Florentine in
English Montreal
dispensing Ukiyo-e prlnts
for this or that occasion
sunsets over sofas
Bernini's plaster "Chase"
Hermes on the stairs pitched
on one talaria a
hot-dog god...

batchman traveller
in drygoods saint or
saintless immigrant your
future was the thing
a change of slides and
you're in paradise
Canada your fresco
seven children with florid
Edwardian names a
wife of lofty innocence
a scientist for God
a trailblazer

your favourite dead in France
you vowed to keep in touch
fell back on the link
between occult and
the metaphysic of wealth
did it shake you
leave you more serene
league of black-haired women
Blavatskys groping for
your pocketbook weaving
sharpness round your
geniality

when you posed at Luxor
as a sheik when you graced
canoes as ballast
charmed enormous salmon
into your empire did
something stain your ton
sting your vest
a claw unlatch your hat
to program boom then bliss
bliss then blindness?

Above the living and the dead—
a riverbed of stars, planets,
red and distant in relational
curves. I would like that special sound,
something so distinct that I might
sit in bars on one-time disaster
days and not be overcome by
the sadness of thc exhausted,
or the early bluster of the
newest breed of world possessors.

The moon is up, a drifting cat's
paw covering its face—on blots
of grey the the instant spoor of tracers
may have marked the day successful—
and as I represent the flux,
the play, the actual flow,
you may feel this moon, the atom,
Dogstar, Phoenix, everlasting stray
of light, the liquid consequence
of sudden memorial pain.

The element of stillness bears
the rattle of a train, dumb cry
of voices, helices of flies.
Exaggerate the poet's claim
for silences!   Place reticles
against the billion-terraced glass
of our inheritance! I know
the rigid preachers' "peace" restrains
that greater truce when we survive
the relevance of our survival.

Across the lake the careful greens
are plastered with expended light.
The moon, grown shriller, bobs away
on islands of synthetic snow.
My care, my joy exonerates
the shadows from the crime of their
detachment—tomorrow though the
twin cause of winner and loser
and paralyzing words about
the full-face warriors and saints.

Point St. Charles (Fragments)

Between the abattoir and the canal
Live all the rogues and the wonderful liars,
Youngsters who can remember dropping
Like reckless birds from the massive lift bridge,
Old men who can recall in the original
Grammar of the "Pint", wild horses bucking
In the fine corral of Stewart's horse yard, or
A winter sleigh race down Napoleon road.

Athletes are legendery heros of
The Point: hockey players, paddlers from the
Boating Club, the mighty men who played an
Indian game so terrible that it was
Outlawed. In photographs you see them stretched
Supine, each hair in place, or dreaming off
In rigid contraposto, or kneeling
Stiffly striped along a war canoe. And
Nothing but the Irish names conveys a
Menace, conjures up the happy mayhem
Of Lacrosse, the fine exhuberance of
Boiler-makers at their play. Just how much
History has been 'borried' from the facts
Is now, and was, impossible to say.

Cut off by the canal, dyked behind the
Railroad, the Point is like an island, a
Tundra of occupations, a climate
Of work and lay-off, an asphalt canvas
Spread over the meadows. Facing the light
Uncertainly, the old rows of two or
Three storey grey and rose-red houses stand
And wait, as horses wait for the bull's charge.
Close by the river off Wellington Street,
The park sheds the season's cycles from its
Trees, flanked by the looming muscular glass-
Works, and the elegant vermilion peak
Of a deserted seignory. Churches
Make their integral signs above the roof
Of a half world.

One evening, drinking beer, I overheard
A longshoreman, now retired, and a
Cabdriver and railwayman—retired,
Talking up the "good old days"—just where had
Buffalo Bridge been, and who had married whom
From Griffintown, who was living over
In Goose Village now, who was dead, and who
Was a grandfather, whose boy was foreman
At the Locomotive Works, and who was
Taken off to jail. They must have known the
Lot these two: all the punks and painters,
The carpenters and gamblers, the sailors
And truckdrivers, butchers, yardmen, locksmiths,
Electricians, firefighters, foundry-
Men, politicians and the petty thieves,
Provocative Irishmen, themselves so
Easily provoked, "Bronchos", clownish and
Respectable, puckered Scotsmen always
Whisky-wheezing at some thorny joke, and
All the patient,greying, loyal, loving, wives.

The voice of the Point is the voice of
A clan. It speaks a slang of pathos, an
Argot of righteousness, a sermon of
Slapstick in the face of things. It preaches
Sin and the parables of fate; it rides
Silence and solitude out of a man.
And if you can't take it, brother watch out...

You stupid Dogan, he was the best
Centre player they ever had. The
Coach just didn't like him.

When I was fourteen my old man kicked me out.
Fend for yourself, he says.
He was a mean bastard.

Good morning, ma'm, I'm from the Hydro, he says.
Don't start gettin fresh around here, I told him.

We had a freight car all picked out,
Full of cigarettes, but the gang never
Showed up that night. Maybe they couldn't
Get a car.
The wife sure knew something funny was goin on.

GOLDA

to fix the dates

        would be irrelevant

I was probably

              night you defected from
       eighteen that
           your worldly lover

parked so late outside the

          high paired stairways on
          Crescent Street

                  you said

   "I can't tonight...you understand"

I did — because of

        charmed authority

because you spoke directly and

           in freedom

(for you at least)

        it couldn't last

          — your heady tolerance —

it wasn't worth

        your patience

we wandered

      almost losing track   hitchhiked in the

                                      dust of trucks

                                      wicker grace of

                                      Model Ts

signed

    unlikely names

        in country hotels that were

                          ironed sunlight
                cottony inside
                        laundered boxes

I'd wake up first

    tell you how I felt

        tell you that

Art was outside the window

            that a great painting was

            running free inside me

            like the

hungry river at Varennes

            sense your face receding

            liquid eyes becoming lights

            detached

your still-provoking breasts on the

            bleached paper of

            the walls

       as orange and as deaf...

            as shapely as Tahiti

MOE REINBLATT (PAINTER)

Spices from the Middle East
By way of Russia
Ripened

The Jewish fruit

After all the years
Bursting from its skin

Purple veins
Sections of vermilion
Gilded pips about the core
The juice of
All the summers
That never were

Laid bare

Rosh Hashonah 5717

A silver day
Silver blowing through the trees
I still have
All the luck Moe
Walking at noon
On the Mountain we both celebrate

I think of twenty years ago
I met you
In a still life you were
Painting in the evenings
(I had the studio in the daytime)
It was filled with
Small hard globes of determination
And the promise of orchards

Since then
You have become
Two three or more well known personages
Popping up
With the same amiable countenance
In different parts of the city

There is

Moe Reinblatt sales representative
Moe Reinblatt the husband of Lil
Moe Reinblatt teacher of art
Moe Reinblatt renowned for paintings
Full of a rare
And complicated cookery

I know you at the present time as

Moe Reinblatt great chef
From Saint Joseph Boulevard
Who swallows the taste of colours
Like a goldfish gulping
Who stews the Arab copper
In the dark cellars
Of the old world
Who makes pie crust from the autumn sky
(One part of crisp white
One part crushed blueberries)
And salad from the rabbis' beard
Which is
A flagrant breach of the Law

Who else but you
Could blur the unpalatable white winter
With black compassion

FOLLOWING GOODRIDGE ROBERTS

a party at his place

once found myself trailing Goodridge Roberts
tried to catch up but couldn't it was night and
he was wearing a white suit which was strange along
Saint Urbain past the Sandwich Shop and straight up
Shuter to his apartment where it turned out to be
the father Theodore Goodridge Roberts novelist—
poet and short story writer his face was totally
different a fearful romantic he combed out
the womens' hair calling them darling
later Goodridge laughed we lived like

gypsies he might have said

FROM THE EXHIBITION CANADIAN PAINTING IN THE THIRTIES
THE RED PORTRAIT BY PHILIP SURREY
BLUE NUDE BY GOODRIDGE ROBERTS

The Red Portrait   Blue Nude
         the colours referred to are
BLUE the smoke in basement
         rooms (basement studios)
         Montreal's bohemia if we'd known
         it at the time and
RED Margaret's brick-red sweater
         as she sits on a kitchen chair
         in the slippery corridor the
         trumpet-light of her
         husband's survival

How Could You Cause Such Waiting

How could you cause such waiting
you're not that good,
dry hair, discoloured front tooth;
if it's lasting you're counting on, don't!

I'm a nasty fellow.
I'm due to foreclose some enormous debts.
All my life I've been waiting for someone like you
and I'll be waiting after you've left.

Even the weather's turned back
but you're a rainmaker aren't you, that's your trade,
flaming desserts your special,
throttling clocks into thunderheads.
By God you'd better be good
you'd better be great...

You coming to me me waiting, a farcical act,
bought you a ticket, found you a seat, all but
wiped the egg from your starving mouth.
It's Simenon you should be reading!

The conductor comes through, doddering father steam;
punch and smile, smile and punch.
Just what do you have to rate
such morbid attentions,
my priceless poet's shoulder?

The St. Lawrence

I can never claim it, the River.
Its reaches scatter my most ambitious plans,
Its dimensions are my master, its single sign
Ambiguous, enigmatic. I am a sea-plane
Exiled to the directing sky, insignificant,
A fly on giant street corners.

If I could shave the words of bigness, shatter
The complacent surface like a mammoth fish,
Leaping, shaking the pieces from its back—
But now I see that it is nothing less
Than love that I am asking for

Yet not love of the River but love
Of the river in me, the mauve metal of the water
At Batiscan shares a personal bias as in winter
When memory hibernates in city's labyrinth—
I plead Europe as my defense, weakly rub
My orientated eyes.

But then, attuned again when April comes,
Cocked to hear the finest crack, to catch
Reflections from the first blue-sensitive wounds
In the steaming snow, reveal in lieu of
Human events the distant ice jamming up
Over the road at Pointe du Lac.

LAST DAY AT SEA

You and Peter and I
Wait for the land as the sea
Compels its horizon lions to lie.
A baggy sailor silvers a winch,
And Udette impatiently climbs.
This is the day when a blip
Of violet-blue extends on the screen,
When the pencil line meets printers' black,
And the derricks restlessly flex
From a ten day sleep.

Below us the wedge of the bow
Moves like a juggernaut
Over short salamming waves,
Rides them smoothly and silently down
With only a snapping of the stays
And the ever insistent brake
Of wind which claws at canvas hoods
And whips the raking towers
Into our wake.

This is the gentlest evening
After the storm of
Mountainous hills unhinged and
Running against our side like Ahab's whale.
Flickering lids of grey and pink
Hang dreamers on the rail, and brilliance
Merges the strolling groups
With dark rose-tinted wood.
We ride the strength of turbines
Spinning below in lustrous casings.

First come the drifters
Galley lights ablaze,
Some distant ships just as darkness
Raises the prickly strip. The pace
Becomes processional. We drag
A fiery tail towards the headland's eye
Which cleverer than the rest
First winks at us and then at Lisbon
Round the bluff, clustering
On modest hills.

LOUIS' STORE

Emerging from Louis' store,
The pet shop of the mind,
With a dozen poets under my arm,

I remember his reassuring smile.

Placing them in my captive car
Like so many budgies in a box
Simulating sleep.

"Reading by the lot now," I said—

Then behind the clicking lock
In the cage of home
I let them loose.

I should have asked for instructions.

Soon Cocteau and Apollinaire
Are perched on the bookshelf.
Elliot has assumed an eagle shape.
Thomas' white mouth is open
And is going to speak.
Tennessee Williams is demanding attention in blue.

Couldn't I have asked for just one poet?

Now Rilke is rising from the package
In two volumes.

NERUDA

paired with a nameless Chileno
Neruda has died
combined with his gesture of
jungles freedoms stagnations coastlines heartbeats contritions...

a tireless worker with his red sweatband of words
the corpulent consul of words choking with white erotic leaves

Parral
Parral
the jungle is treated for silence then mystery
sprayed for inceptions and dark incestuousness
a train goes by and neither faction trembles
a train goes by
and no one recalls
its wooden roses   string of clouds
weighing from the branches

the capitals of the world are a single city
to tour the world is to look for some way out
not as it used to be

the exile eating his meals of comfort
can therefore never be exiled
the exile in his light coat and leathery skin
dreaming of how a sun of words once
flooded a Catholic continent
cantos like the firm ground of Chile
were thorn and sand rock and copper veins
if you could break down the door of a poem
capture it deliver it for trial
you'd have the poet
if you could trap his swarm of words and
cultivate its essence
you'd have a sap like mirrors
a sky that clears like sanity and dreams

Section Two

Spain — Mallorca

YOUNG WIDOW

In your case, Maria,
Mourning hardly becomes you;
Black can only contradict,
My lady in tears.
In that contorted face I sense a ritual grief,
A final gesture for the dead.

The source will dry, and cease
To well up harshly in your sentimental songs
How can it be otherwise;
Flowers jostle in the yard, perfect fruit
Abounds along the tough meandering vines,
Place and Paradise are one.

Work. Sleep. Sing.
Drink the sun each day in a clear sweet wine.
Time will do the rest.
Share your food with ants,
Thrill to the masculine stroke of the
Cathedral bell.
That much is permissible!

SUMMER NIGHT

The moon reigns into the dark; a huge
Moist pan of light, soft orange, a pyrotechnic
Peach, cleaves the face of the sea with a path,
The black mercurial deep down where fishes
Flick their flukes unnoticing in the extinguished
Depths. The skull of a Phoenician fills
And fuses with fleshly shells, finds a less
Uncomfortable anonymity—a saintly bone-washed
Second birth and flowering of little cones and
       fans and fins.
Bats tumble in the brambled night.
Rich rocks rear in the theatrical eye.
Cats spring cunningly into thickets of dust,
Snake black through dunes and ditches of
Dimmest light. Dogs bark crazily at the
Echoing walls bobbing with shadows. Lovers bless
With their animal eyes the upturned fragments.
Close-up wanderers lean on a ragged rim.
And wrapped in the cloth of their ruin,
The lonely soldiers loll and straggle, scuff
And crunch, smoke, skulk, scare and scowl
Through the long ordained unmilitary smugglers'
Night, the scented sea-syrupy Mediterranean
       night.
Out along the shoreward road little bar-bodegas
Spell their neon names beneath a web of lights:
The Saint Tropez experiments with girls,
The Burro Blanco, says six languages, 'tea like
Mother used to make and cake,' The California,
The Caroussel, La Cabaña. Music from a borrowed
Record player swings and switches, spills a
Restless lullaby down among the cauliflower rocks.
Lantern faces, lit with the common secret of
The night, pass in search of pleasure ports.
Cheek-to-jowl excursion boats, furled and nested
In the arms of a cosy harbour, slip gently
To and fro with the snoring of the sea.

Time and the moon have risen. It is twelve o'clock.
A single yellow gimlet eye goes black.

MALLORCA

To rid my head
Of the sharpener's whine,
And the still green growing forms,
I stretch my legs and start to walk—
Past the cabbage rocks
And the towering house of cellars,
Stitched with fancy iron locks.

Out beyond
The orchard grove
Goggled spearmen
Sprawl upon the syrup sea;
Sunburnt Saturday heroes strut
Until the clock's croak—
But for me

Time is two
Brown shoe toes that beat
Beside the clinging peacock's garden,
That pass the peak
Of gypsies' ambush,
That pace the long
Inviolate wall

Of almonds;
Underneath the bridge of threes
Round the cottage corner, to strike
At bravely bobbing bay,
Where I, a sailor of
A different sort,
Cut sapphire signals from the breeze,
Tack smartly by the tower clock,
And with my captain's choice,
Tease out a strip of saffron flag
To kiting over Eden Rock.

Larry's

Like rotten fruit channeled
In the direction of purgatory,
    The most hilarious buffoons
Of 'to hell with it', gather
    In plenary session one to a perch.
"Where' s old Wally?" somebody bawls.
    Oh you've really got to be there,
It's a panic! In a white coat,
    Sober and sadly, stands Larry—
Living up to his role of convener,
    Confessor and tail-end boy
The last conceivable messenger, the
    Man nobody asks out to dinner.
And nobody would if they knew
    He fires buck-shot into each tropical
Beak as it opens up to yawp
    And confronts every squashy smile
With a terrible sign saying: death DEATH.
    "Whadllya do with all these
Toothpicks Larry, build an extension?"
    "No sir, I'm thinking of building
A coffin especially for you,
    A labour of love sir." Say
Are you writing a poem, or something
    About bars? You'd better be careful,
Drinking's an institution round here.
    Anyway look who's talking about
Other people, this poem of yours
    Doesn't even rhyme.

FISHERMEN

Men who have grappled at dawn
With an old giant lolling in their nets;
Who is to tell them there is no longer something
In the unique way they bear the strain,
In the way they gouge out a chunk of bread
With their short silver knives?

Who is to tell them about our aversion to
The strong mellow salt smell of fish?
Who is to point out the idiocy of all
That patching and mending?

The sea of the stories we know, is a
Pleasure lake, a challenge to eccentric amateurs,

No place for clumsy sails and blunt wooden boats
With four cylinder motors.

What thrill is there for a young man
In the apologetic kick and cough
Of these old timers?

PROCESSION — HOLY WEEK

As darkness falls
Like failing vision,
Led by three white horsemen
The spool of the procession
Commences to unwind;
Threads up a narrow lane,
Through the starting archway,
Beside the tinted houses,
Down,
And into the town.

In the plaza
Waiting to punctuate:
Are the floats, a black
Virgin with a fussy halo, and
A troup of soldiers,
Gun butts up in mourning;
As the lamps go bobbling past
And down—
The candles and the
High pointed caperuzas,
Penitential thorns.

Time trembles equivocally.
The little square enacts its
Tale of occupation.
Goya looks up at the windows
For his forms, women
Leaning on the narrow rails
Against a yawn of tone.
He starts to think about aureolin.

The Virgin wobbles out
Into the stream of points,
And a solemn dead march
Carries her awav.
So many faithful
Passing in Thy sight, Lord,
So many still in Thy
Mysterious keeping.

ELUARD WRITES POETRY

he proved he
could do it without
naming names his face
composed like the solar vanes on
a satellite

well not quite

a sheathing of irreverance
a smoothed-by-pleasure look and
irony not innocence

innocence is closed
and he was not

words he strung together like a
peasant for a Book Of Songs
urban peasant
springfed with words
earthy with culture

there were deadly choices in his way
but he
was vague enough and real enough to
make the right one as a poet

fatal chores he accepted as part of
the paradox of light —
a marriage of Art and Resistance (black
eclipsing white in the public mind
but not in his)
                        again he
seldom — if ever — laid charges

his face as I said was polished and poised
like a sun collector
a grid for enriching the flux by
a single vital degree

perilous mix of the here and the far

the fiction of artless (timeless) delight
thought as its mindless sod

the faction of our animal
our heavenly
involvement

NIGHT OF THE TOURISTS

The eight o'clock night
Is black morphine
For the plaza.

The plaza is parched
And dying of its
Usual faces.

Soon sirening neon
Swallows the footsteps
And tourists.

With a puff of silver
The moon of eleven
Scatters the black
Seeds of night.

Not knowing poems,
The dog and his shadow
Pass urgently by,
Ahead of the morning

SAN ANTONIO DE LA FLORIDA

Goya is buried here
Beside the tracks.
Here in dry crêpe-paper forms
He serenades Madrid.

Faceless figures incline
Toward each other
Insinuating.
Nothing is sure
Except the softest red
And yellow of wine.

And here — about these walls —
The worldless game of art
Flourished
Like a flower in concrete,
Only a rifle shot
From the agony of the University.

In Memory Of Garcia Lorça

Garcia Lorca,
Did you think
They'd let it go,
A flower in the lapel
Of perpetual mourning?
Did you guess
The brilliant words
Had made you alien
And (strangely)
Evil?

Granada let you die
Like any freak;
Forgot the day,
Forgot which pit it was.

Gypsies, farmers, generals,
Priests, tourists,
And the quiet rich,
Now pass blandly
Overhead.

Oiga hombre!
Ask around.
Somewhere,
Buried,
Is a silver skull.

SPAIN 1955

1

Don't ask about the Civil War in Spain!
I did, and felt
The iron differences again,
The old wound never quite scars up,
The rigid joint can still
Fill up with pain.

2

The predatory birds,
      In patent-leather hats,
That walk the night in pairs
Remind me that man
Is the supreme bird of prey.
The ugly buzzard can be shooed away.

FOR BROCK — MY BROTHER

Yesterday, and when the nisperos hung
In honey-coloured drops, this was your garden.
The neat little fruit trees are my hosts today.
And the vines approach with their most
      tender shoots.
For once I wish I knew the names of all these plants.
The spiky one has reddish scarlet blooms,
And something grows too innocently blue against
      the wall.
A pine tree puffs above the sun-white rooms.
The bougainvilla is decimated in the heat.
You must have seen the peaches turning
      softly into fall.

La Maison Natale De Picasso

The place where Pablo Picasso was born is number thirty-six
on the third floor in the Square of Mercy (power, discretion),
a model of the age, five neat tiers of oven doors
on white plaster, sand-domes stencilled in the sun's quicklime.

In the afternoon of its usefulness it stares out without
benefit of trees (a note on the painter said that these
were fortunate times, although 'the incident' happened here).
Having no glass, the windows reflect a blaze of interior coolness.

From the firm white shaddocks of his mother's breast
the artist here received his first instruction, and if her dress
closed all to the neck — the slightly ovaled eyes the firm catholicity
'If someone were to tell me you had sung the Mass...'

Hardly unfortunate to be born in Malaga (in a town whose top
looked off to where the sea lay negligently, weighed blue across
the palisade of palms) sister oval-eyed, father like a stick of shade,
waves of fashion coming down the line from Barcelona.

Judgment Day

A trumpet note
Tremulous and thin
The seven old men file in
Expecting peace or pain.
       It is not so much a question
       Of faith as one of feeling.

In polished black
Around each veined foot
The sun spins back
A yellow silence.
       It is not so much a question
       Of faith as one of feeling.

Radiantly naked
The dignitaries rise
In whose oval eyes
The splintered colours spawn.
       It is not so much a question
       Of right as one of living.

Condemned to live again
The seven young men
Quiver in a shock of green
The irresistible second spring.
       It is not so much a question
       Of faith as one of feeling.

Section Three

VIEW FROM THE HILL

Strangely taut,
held with ineffable poise,
the evening hangs for an instant
like your question,
      ready to slide exhausted
      down the windowpane,
to roll its glinting eye once and for all
      in a parody of death.

No one can argue
with such a time.
The air is eggshell thin
and time wears a piqued look
      like your lovely face.
      The factories underneath
the hill have lost their muscle of smoke,
      that acquisitive bulge.

This is perhaps how we
should live, uncommitted,
tight as string, spare as saints
between the two extremes.
      Smile if you like—
      but here is some of
the poet's wish; the fine edge of your profile,
      the abstract of my love.

THE OCEAN—JACKSONVILLE

The ocean is always exciting, now
Misty grey stampeding past the land.
The sea is my element; its pale iridescence
My choice, its beneficent blue my Riviera,
As a boy, my solace
On the wide St. Lawrence.

I turned my back on the sadness
Of northern shore; on the land parental,
The four-square crudeness
Of those along its length, to know
The water's smooth release, its sparkling edge,
The ships that crawled beneath
Towers of smoke.

I knew before I was there;
The Mediterranean, the orange coast of Sardinia,
The sweet amorphous way of the South—
A life so like the river,
Changing, luminous, flowing,
Deep in the eye, in the
Fine graffiti of hair.

Its fluid mark is mine;
The ocean streaming, armies of porpoise grey
By Jacksonville. Not even a moon
Can fix its gift, or sermon
Give it sense. My back is to the land
Set as the oldest idea—unyielding,
A Puritan rock
In the gentle currents that flowing
Can form a heart.

This is the river, the thing of importance
Smudging in the heat, slurring
The definitions of bank, edge, beach, point, curve.
The islands are narrow, grassed-over flats
Pointing—pointing into the current. A few
Cattle are scattered about, and that's all.

Can you imagine anything happening here:
Blue and white coated soldiers in flat-boats,
Dirty Indians, their faces ribbed with grease,
Melting toward the church spire, the small
White half-moons of the martyrs' eyes
Beseeching?

Now, listless in the grip of a dreary tenancy
The land stretches away. Occasional tin roofs
Which are its ancient eyes, water in the sun.
Who will come and ravish the dreaming slut? Who
Will bring sharpness and distinction as his gift?

Is this he, the ship, mosaic on the lead, indifferent
To the slow turn of events, unaware of the myths
Which have made the dog with its wagging tail,
The true seigneur?

For Marino Marini

It is the portrait heads
That are sure to appeal to a writer;
Old sharply expressive faces with the sun in their eyes
As the sun is in the open windows of my house today.
Men wise enough to love their vices
With their virtues. Warmth and age favour flesh,
But bone is bone nevertheless.
The nudes are Pomona—the essential female fruit,
The ripe uncertain form surrounding a buried seed.
And last, or first, are the riders, astride
Their anthropological mounts, all sinew and outward thrust—
Marini the man, who has learned to grunt
And cry out his joy
In a radiant consciousness.

Goodbye Mrs. F. . .
Out of Glasgow into — where?
Since you have left the directory,
        since the expressway
Has changed
The character of your place,
And your memory shot, a disgrace.
(Is that how you went?)
        Let me at least
Ask protection from those swankier graves,
A comfortable rebate (from whom,
The Great Tax Collector?)
                on business still
                        pending.
Perhaps you already lie like a dove
In the square beards' lawn.
Perhaps you are drunk,
                if so
May the whisky be strong and superdistilled.
When you wake
                may the blinds be drawn,
May your lining be stiff
With ten dollar bills.

Goodbye Mrs. F. . .
Wherever you are.
        Wherever you go
My wishes go with you,
                you glorious raconteur.
No drawing-room portrait is truly authentic
Without a note
        appended by you:
"That old Mr. P. . used to like to —
The meatiest part of the Bluebook
        is under your blowsy hair.

But this is unkind,
        I should say
That many a pious elder turned to a goat
In the sizzling hush of your kitchen.

How did it go? —
The stairway door to the right,
                 the sideboard,
(Which of them left you that?)
The tumblers set out in the light
Like a glowing compact
Between us.
Goodbye Mrs. F. . .
Your maxim;
"A thing worth doing is worth
                          doing well,"
Has been the comfort of two generations of
Devious gents. And curse — "dirty buggers!"
You said of the rest.
                 Should our meeting
Be counted a lapse in this happy progression
Or blessed default?
                 For if you had offered
To 'freshen' for me,
                 Or queried professionally,
"Are you athletic?"
My expression, my dear Mrs. F. . ..
Could have strained our mutual tact,
Doubled your "thirty-five" years
            The truth, you kindly old souse,
                          that I entered your place
As a blight on the family tree,
As the ardent poet —
                          (but how could you know,
An ethical louse.)

Goodbye Mrs. F. . .
Sober or drunk
                    may you always succeed.
May the wealthier classes continue to breed.
                    But then
Have you died? Have they walled you up
In some institution?
Did the shadowy F. . . come home?
                              If not
May your new address have a phone
Which can only ring for a pedigreed voice.
May it never
Find you alone.

POLICE STATION

Choose up sides!
Puffy lidded cop
Or brace of golden farmer boys,
Storing summer in shirts and sinews,
Suppliant in handcuffs.

No one loves the slaughterhouse attendants.

Decorate the detective
Sweating in the ordering phone,
Bullying out the necessary facts;
No brawling blood,
No crumple of fear,
No fuddle, no guns, no knives.

Recognize the desk man,
A minor diety, placated with
Pocket handkerchiefs, keys and coins,
Performing the liturgy
Beautiful in categories
On the dark river bank.

Salute the fading pair
With a bravado wink.
Rise with relief as the curtain stuns
The first faint yelp.

How did it come to you,
Like a slate hill in the blue blade
Of the Arctic day, or piecemeal;
Full, chalk, loose-fitting skins,
The dog-toothed grins
Bristling with fur,
Gift of your unsmiling friends, walrus or seal?
Great hunter! The masks of your superiority!
What have you to fear but truth,
The ugly iron boat which each year
Left invisible lances like the sun's rays.
(The snow torn with sudden blood—
Your blood this time.)
But to get back you saw them
As they were in the oil-lit igloo,
Their mouths smeared with seal oil,
Their bodies known to you,
Held by you
In the half seen miracle of human tenderness.

A 'North Country' Accent

I used to like
Your north country accent.
You said "land" as if
You'd just baked it in the oven,
And "love" as if you had it
Cupped in your hand.
There was always a glow of familiarity,
I swear your voice could reach out
And touch me on the arm.

A mystery deepened when you walked,
Or stood contemptuously
At the stove,
                    and it was pure sorcery
When you lay in the cleft of that old sofa.

I think you turned shyly away
From your own fierce whiteness,
From the shocking vigour of those three dark spots.

POEM

What is my imagination? Is it
Sense of size or menace? Why
Should 'seagrape' strike me magic as
A gift? Is it song or generations
Sounding? Am I the farthest one in time
To stumble on a word's accretion—
A unicorn's becoming?

Why is smoke beyond the trees
A presence? Is it height, because it
Moves? Is it stories told a thousand times
Through heavy lion beards, enjoined
With love's unfolding? Is it dying too?
Must it wither like the wealth
Of man's perverse believing?

Can we replace a minotaur
Each life by something quickly made
Of opposites? Are we proof against the
Chestnut blossoms standing every spring,
The mixing sound of water in the roots
Reviving wanderings as odd as making
Kings and beasts of all we knew?

Histoire Baroque

Land of lands
And still more mellow
Lands of time; the slow arctic
Turn of change uncovers its devotees.
Sepalled buds recalling climate, place,
And course sprouting in the
Perfumed fields. I who seemed in love,
Invoke the first chimeric stage;
A deaf enchantment from the sea,
Cartwheels spinning high above the bells
And cinder parapets,
Scissors, splits, and silences applaud
The sun who daily rides
The stately bullring of my eye.

What else was there to learn?
To say that life is beautiful,
Not to shout or run or throw a stone,
To brush the pools of emerald baize,
To lie beneath the pressing midnight mauve
And feel the branches graze
As fingers fondle in the dawn.
Raddle of the blood, baboons
Which profile to your questioning.
Music made from birds that fan and bicker
On the dreaming sill.
Every carelessness transfixed
On three dark stars, the avalanche
Which calls itself beloved.

At thirty years
Pleasure probes a singular ontology;
("Know the why and wherefore."
Said Beaudelaire recovering from hasheesh)
Wisps of wind for solid domes,
A jaunty scaffolding which
Summers in the waves, caging for an instant
Blaze of fish, showers slanting for the land,
Yards of brassy kelp,
Drift and drag, nothing valued
By the world.
Titles catch against the angular supports,
Puffs from passing trains unravel
Through a wall of strings.

The next is unexpected;
Cramps and couplings, snowflakes
Frozen in the summer sky, white cocoons
Where each one still as death
Awaits his spring and only
Words will strike against the tinder air.
All about my mountain school
Silence gavels in a curse,
Ensor masks make Saturday parades
(superstition routed by the threat of white)
Aglomerate above the newly live,
And like the pious Magi
Prod for roses
In an anxious face.

At first the word
And then the inarticulate night,
Sight without the coloured distillates of flame,
Light for the harlequin
Touching his lips goodbye, turning —
Making a last slow turn.
A Japanese with a great
Proclivity for snow; he too
feels the second immaculate glow,
The Holyland of no return,
And yet he sings exquisitely,
A snowsinger tipped against the wind
On a vanishing road.

Words,
Pipe, piano, drum, and flute—
No professional music here,
Invention, and the crystal blood
Empiric in a single note, each one crypto-cloaked
Against a flattened space. Who
In all the world knows the musicmaker's mind,
The meaning of his eloquent charade?
One eye a sun, and one
The smoky bud of blindness,
His soaring hat of plume
Mistaken for the king himself.

Man fantastic,
The sum of his adaptions;
Crutched against the tidal pull,
Clawed and crabbed, puffed,
And fitted out of all imagining, and still
Imagines oneness in his self.
Worships fruit with its august centre,
Sees extremity of red and green,
Freedom parlayed to a bitter fortune;
The cyclic prophecy fullfilled — eclipse,
And Moon, the ancient queen,
Reclaim her children
From the stinking cabal of defeat.

On Sitting Between Two Young Stars Of The Ballet Russe

I didn't have time to feel unnerved
Just lent back slightly on my stool
Letting the Russian get through
Much too close to stare I used
Peripheral vision body radar

The counter stretched from door to door
Of Liggett's Drugs next door to
Branchaud's barber shop which was next
To His Majesty's Theatre these girls
Had the vivid projection of stars
Stopping the lunchtime rush
Talking gravely together being
Entirely conspicuous

And there was the pressing matter
Of sex (I was nineteen at the time)
Of sensibility one was black and white with
A floppy hat and the other a chestnut brunette
Of bodies and all that control
Theatre and beautiful lightheartedness
Expressed through ART
My deathless religion...

I passed two serviettes
One to the left and one to the right
Got back a turbulent broken TOUMANOVA
A closely curled BARONOVA with only
A nod at my existence
The slightest break in their conversation

Once I Was Dirty

once I was dirty
bad wine sloped across my jackets
I worked at my art 'til my eyes blurred
lusted for women
lay exhausted in the sad
high sarcophagi of rented rooms

I tutored a nervous dropout
from the garment industry fell for
a girl who hated sex with
all her being drank six
cups of coffee in the morning bruise
of light and continuation

inexperienced I was the
great believer as the city's
good grey slush rose to my ankles I was
its skin its purple breath
its pupa and its low-born child

in the bleak extravagance of
being young I tasted parties with a
gourmand's palate choked on the charms
of my sisters carried
the one face back to my rooms
racked and luminous as love's delay

Poem In Praise Of S.

you're up I see
naked and busy
with half my life still clinging about you
(water round a swimmer)

mother what infinite lightness
the tusk of hist'ry painlessly extracted
continents restored

FRIGHTENED OF SNAKES?

to hell with JAWS and
snakes and hairy tarantulas
It's Pontiacs we should be scared of
Cadillacs Chevrolets
Frontenacs (extinct Canadian
breed I know my parents had one)

think of this special list —
        Frank O'Hara
        Jackson Pollock
        David Smith
        our own Red Lane
        Oscar Cahan
        Camus —
just sitting in the back a passenger!
Absurd way to end

at seventeen I had a friend who seemed
to *need* a crash crossed Victoria
Bridge at 2 a.m.

reasoned with him pled
then climbed in back and tried
to slow him by
wringing his neck

83 miles per hour that's the
last check I made a tree in the
front seat where I formerly sat
(a poplar probably ten times my age)

and it's me that bled —
red stuff seeping from somewhere
putting out my cigarette

dripping splinters of glass
standing in the middle of the road
in the riddle of the night
with all the beauty I owned
with all the living I'd do
then and forevermore

FATHER

I come from the shoots of your middle time
the burrowing guilt;
fly or crash it taught me
I did neither of these.

I'm going to retire your line
of beautiful teeth,
there isn't room for us both.
It's perfect that nobody sings
in my background and
laughter can't be performed; I warned you
a poet's a SERIOUS MAN
a conductor of SERIOUS TRENDS.

I like the advice of your three
last words which were, "aw shut up."
But truly you made me speak to your
terrible dunce's joy,
'shut up' was what you couldn't hear and never heard
the width of an ear that was crawling
with demons or roaring with outrage or
prim as an empty space
or slicked to your head
with formless satisfaction.
Wonderful state.

Of course I couldn't speak for
a single second of your childhood, your role
as rover, star of soaring goals—
punching Killer in the face with
provident strength. *

              And I
couldn't verify the tale that
you were detained as a spy
that you once loved somebody or telephoned
a whisky-swilling whore
who called me Charles (your name) and asked,
"Are you athletic like your father?"
"Yes and no," I said, but she'd
forgotten the question

Yes and no to all the things
you stood for, all the things that
print so cleanly from your fading negative.

*   Austin Killer was the name of my father's opposite number in the
junior OHA championship at Stratford in 1905. They were both rovers.
        From the Stratford Herald of 1905, "Grier hit Killer a blow on the
face, Killer was wise and didn't retaliate."
        During these same championship games the Toronto Star said he
was unquestionably the best junior player ever developed in Toronto."
        In 1920 he became the amateur golf champion of Canada.

I Was Brought Up by the Sea
For Istvan Anhalt

I was brought up by the sea
I felt that I'd never lose its weedy taste its garden in my hair
I used to examine it with primitive instruments
proving truth or so I thought

I'd touch its poisoned cold
but my counterspell was more than adequate
sea in which rails are engulfed
in which iron breaks an egotistical silence.

I once saw something drowned
and it had losts its name
white with exceptional legs it was growing out of the rocks.
I knew nothing of tragedy

confront me and I always broke. I'd become habituated.
If I claimed a city it grew bulbs across the roofs
it chopped the streets I chose like a chromium guillotine
head from body body from head
I was innocent and rich   I even felt as if
the sea were looking for me...

2

what should we domesticate
what should we contaminate with our ideology
the sea with paws withdrawn cats paw sphinx paw
the wonderful arm machine of water
I ask you
has the alphabet died
is there a single word which doesn't respond
like servants torn from sleep...

I lived in the soil of my senses glowing and disassembled
the fisherman's boat the chambered-heart indenting was my music
the fog was my night
my punctuation ships as thin as wafers
open mouth and royal ears I came to the sea
in its packing case of stones
its grainless cut across the day
I played the North like a empty card
I read the sun like a broken seismograph

3

through stillness what have we presumed
why have we not created from our emptyness
here was the sea's effluvium sharp ad explicit
the rhythmic threshing of stones
was itself an ageless application...

through my personal bead of glass I played examiner
recording the passing of names
voiceprints on the oyster of the sky...

from the linear shadow explorer's brass
from the cliff of my uncle's house from its shins its ankle
its grizzled toes
from the fly-blue wedge of the land
the hunter hunted the sulphurous detente...

who claims us who cuts us from his will

I was brought up by the sea

its vast anatomy of weight
a list erasing names
rictus   holy   gape

RAVEL

through the wall to my right rock-music
my candy-craving wife beating a pot
of fudge   the dog has
farted again — indescribably
a program honouring Maurice Ravel
L'Indifferent being sung by Maureen Forrester
neon concert image the diva next door
near-perfection in a crumbling age

Debussy on Ravel   the flawless ear
a sick Ravel on himself   no more pleasure
in the making I have failed
am second-rate...music as a language
this beautiful idea has used me
is inadequate
                        and incidentally a
tradition had popped up in France
of bourgeois tinkerers   engineers
in the new tradition of metals and gasses
invention as escape from
words and class and paper emasculation
and historical art
the father building his two cylinder motor
was the son composing music
both transitionalists   both
preparing for flight
nomads   lightweight glidermen
                        ornithopterites

WEDDING DAY

on the day of my wedding
I woke up firm as a midnight doorknob
I ate breakfast of coffee and eggs
that tasted good   my shoes my
shirt and my suit laid out the night before
looked as if they wanted to go through with things

the light of day was my private estate
(never dreamed it could be otherwise)
whatever incidents the
streets had planned were cancelled
I knew that the
church was waiting that sooner or later
the preacher would take me in tow fussed in his role
as slack expatriate of ceremonies

I travelled the route in my
suit which was formal but not too stiff
my shirt of whitest cotton   my shoes shone up
from a piece of hardened polish   the church
had birches in its grey oasis   and it
had me in its balanced ledger   I felt
it was going to tick me off
in the life column   I wanted to open its doors
to blow out the odor of wax and comfortable sanctity
I wanted to show it the streets
of Prussian blue and igloo bricks of red...
my responses (unplanned) were low and flat as
I was the word that day   we were the word
on the day of my wedding
the relatives kept their distance like
frozen extras in a Fellini movie
my best man tall and grave gave
me the gift of some private desolation
on the day of my wedding you stood
out white and uncamouflaged at my side   and
you trembled like life in a trap

Section Four

Section Four

AN ECSTASY

1

Now the first condition is comfort;
and none of the gods could survive
this first condition.

Man must be prodigious, magical and just—

from now on

the poet will work in the bank
and the banker will write poetry,
to his own astonishment.

Craving fullness of life
we have fashioned
a clean blackness;
                    inexplicable

                              expanding
out of the broken shape
of the past.

Closeness has become an infinity
purity has turned to spawning cells—

we are at the beginning.

Without regrets

look up at the colourless dark
that may soon become as familiar to us
as the green of grass.

Look about at our blue-bound world,
at the gentle rivers flowing like smoke,
at the women, young and erect,
at the marvellous invitation
of their breasts.
                    Life must come from their life.
And beauty risk rebirth in strange surroundings.

2

In this city
where the flowers are prisoner
and the sea-porcupine a Gothic myth,

streets are widened, and immediately
the past flows out—
                a golden stagnant water.

Corners are straightened,
and old associations
lost forever.

There is a sadness in this...
we seem to be losing and losing
when in reality we are gaining.

We cannot as yet recognize the
expression of our happiness contained
in the clean new shapes.

But it is there and more.

Let us declare museums, and preserve
what was finest and most characteristic,

and let us build as we feel we must.

3
The long misery
            with its stirring miracles
is coming to an end;

its answered prayers,

its prayers answered.

Festivity and penitence—
with a few elegant exceptions,
and the grizzly Horsemen
clattering out of the sky.

4
Go down to the market
and see the great red and white carcasses
hanging in the cold rooms.

(Meet the farmer and his family.

Their nationality is the country,
ours is the city.

            It makes a difference.

Their complexions are different,
their manner is more open.)

You'll find eels and tobacco for sale,
and if you're lucky,
                        rows of flowers

out on the street;

            four-seasons, and roses,
                        small foster roses,
geraniums and snapdragons,
                            greens,
and mums; white, bronze and lavender, set
against the umber richness of the vegetables.

Imagine to yourself a festival,
a day,
with fresh cut flowers everywhere
in the grey streets.

                5
This lively morning

the young surveyors are warbling like Italians,
and the first wasp moves spastically over
ashen winter grasses.

The great vista of the freight-yard is an enigma
I leave to my children.

Conspicuous for their absence are gondolas
in the crooks of the old canal.

Loving praise, a schoolgirl reads aloud beside
the bubblegum machine.
"His strong arms were about her.
'You shall not go back into the chest tonight!'"
(A perfect age for a traditionalist, I think.)

The blackbirds have peacock feathers on their backs.

Bright red burns coarsely at the foot of
a grave.

A bald man, surely walking for his health, asks
eagerly, "How far before I get a view?"

Bottle caps and shoelaces, things that have
survived the bottom of the white winter's well
receive my entire admiration.

          Paradox, and the world unstitched for a new lacing.

6.

I stir in the white sheets
half awake,
the city round me like a lava bed.

I erect the tall shadows of chimney stacks.

I lay streets that are exclamations of silence.

Energetic white puffs of sound appear.

An engine starts
and stops,

Revolving robot rods clank
along the prongs of a fork.

Stars curve, proffering a frigid joy;

The night about my bed like a pool

7

My feelings are lost without the
                        gold beating of the sun,
caught up in some ancestral web.

I love, but love means reaching downwards,
a breathless blackout in the human nest,

The French-Canadian perpetually *en famille*,
and the Jew who tends the gardens
of his rich black wound —
                    must know a greater unity.
The sky must pass outside a window pane,
outside the curtains snugly drawn together.

It might help if I said
that the sun is essential light, that
the sky passes directly through my eyes
                                making silence,
meeting no obstruction. No primaeval image
stops the way with an imperious sign.

My dear friends, you who have been so kind,
if I turn to stone it is only for a while

until I climb above the hampering walls
to where there is abundant light,
                              and look down for a spell
with the yellow sight of the sun.

                    8
This morning I looked for a poem, "Saltimbanques."

It had disappeared

as so many things are soon to disappear.

If you hurry
          to Europe
you may be in time to give a handout to the last beggar,
to see a king on his charger.
You may find nomadic street-performers in
some out-of-the-way place; the thin sad acrobats
of Picasso,
          and gypsies,
facing extinction like a tribe of aborigines, as
slack and incorrigible as ever.
You may feel there is nothing more moving than
fishermen pushing off from the sand in their curving boats,

and these will be the last to go.

But go they must, like old trees coming down,
like music from the streets.

And for a while
there will be greyness
and confused improvisation.

We shall feel outrage and despair at the sight
of our lives

until we recognize a new beauty
growing up about us, something less harrowing

and ornate — more serene,
lighting up the streets
                                 with clear slabs of colour.

But there is no need to explain.
It has its standards already,

you know what I'm talking about —

music, coming from the most unlikely places,
like new blood,

black and white, full of vitality.

       9
Quebec was a fortress

and the black cannons still wait
on their tracks above the church spires,
commanding the approaches
to the close packed town within the walls.

At the top of Cape Diamond,

stretched out on the grass, I find a bigger
context for this hub of rock.
My daydreaming projects far beyond
the trajectory of any cannon.

It is all the same to me whether
I look up at the steep side or down.

Without a password I stroll about the streets

finding new answers to the plain arithmetic
of the windows, saluting the young women sweeping
in the doorways, invading the dormers
with unmilitary personages.

My rank is above rank.

I take the Governor's Garden for my own.

It was mine long before it was his.

I offer this poem in support of my claim.

I inform the newspapers
                             that it is not for sale.
It cannot be bought any more than one can buy
a garden in the sea.

The first clear day of a cold spring brings
six of us to Quebec

in high spirits.

The terrain is as sensational to us as it
was to the generals.

We find beauty shorn of doubtful motives.

                    10
By the twenty-sixth of May

the leaves are in small clusters,

the grass is emerald green beneath
the bell-cast eaves — in strips across the saddle of the hill.

Figures in the niches of an old church
have been painted gold

against a hurrying overcast

the lime wash whites seem crisper than ever before
in their long history.

Three slender islands, I notice, are still awaiting
the explorers;
                    the vermilion of a spirited people.

Slippery, fresh cut logs are ochre and black,
and the apple trees,
                             astonishing orange flames.

They are straightening the sharpest corners
of the road.

The new cement plant covers farm land
down by the river's edge.
Its grey chimney brushes the sky
                          with two rosettes.
No one ever thought of so much industry.
Spring, and something more.

11

Prophecies are stated in grey and white.
Spells are stacked in the public libraries

without fanfare

forecasts arrive every instant,
                    smaller than pepper seeds.

Gases burn with a wavering hiss
in the lovers' night

rock becomes light and sand becomes glass

and still we are cheated
of time and enchantment.

12
Have patience.

No matter how unsympathetic, how intractable
and fantastic things appear,

we shall eventually claim them for our own.

It has always been this way.

We shall envelope all structures and constructions,
all machines, and the whistling shapes of speed
in our customary joy.

We shall become accustomed to revelations.

We shall welcome surprise as no surprise—
as the sun comes up each day a quivering gold.

We shall invest function with the
fresh colours of our new materials.

Our plainness can only lead to fantasy.

13
I watch my daughter at her swimming lesson
in a green tiled pool.

Her favorite playground,

the sly mercurial water
fills up with pouting shapes;
whorls, splashes, and the
underwater explosions of the divers.

Action is continuous

and grotesque;

feet disappearing, round coloured heads
breaking the surface,
children crouching, falling, shouting, grimacing,

holding their noses.

I intrude on a populous world
of Hieronymous Bosch.

14
More than most people,

the artist

is afraid of the gold gone from his eye
and the plum coloured tendrils grown
where once a god had sat transfixed.

He may feel something great and close to nothing,

a rare expanse of innocence.

To be lost is perhaps to stumble
                                    on the Garden.

It has always been there
even before the first dramatic reporting.

How revealing it would be to find

carved into the trees

the signs and hearts of those who have known
its incomparable spell.

15
I can only sense what lies ahead;

the blue ceiling of Padua — but black,

glowing walls, a pure memory of southern flowers,

poems of the insatiable emptiness.

And for our comfort
and entertainment
resounding from undreamt-of distances,

the tiger-hissing, lion-roaring banter of actors.

16
Sensible is the label which most suits us—

especially the men

who lay great stock in honesty and good sense.

It never amounts to a passion
but you can see it on them,
                              a fine grey pencilling.

As a poet I need to experience ecstasy.

(English poetry never went crazy, a Frenchman said.
It was not a compliment.)

Our poets must give themselves to a kind
of unsensible madness;
they must hear music not meaning as they write.

Words must be clear bells,
or sound gravely along like horns.
They should detonate, explode like lightning
                              under the sea,
be silver wire, silk thread suspended,

sardonyx,

layers of white alternated with sard.

There are words that are the incomparable beasts
                                    of our imagination.

Sound them.
Revel in the extravagance.

I wish to make literature, you say.

Oh, if only we could.

          17
The greens are heavy,
                    almost tropical this summer
because of all the rain.

I see the second country of the seasons;

in a housefly, bright as a bloodstone,

in the dead white face of a woman
                              whose mouth
is a crushed carnation.

18

The river is blue

and gutters are generally grey.

Even here where the city squats
                    and performs its functions,

the odour of grease
is nowhere as strong as the summer's sweetness.

How would you like this city for your lover,
Apollinaire, sick ancient satyr,
                    could you succeed
where the bitter boys have failed,
dead poet of the rose decomposing,
singer of a sadness studded with chimney pots?

Would you win

where the terrible smile of the mayors has spoiled,
where the profiteer grows odd and crooked
in his suffocating morning-coat...

the wedding having been indefinitely postponed?

There is an exhibition of sculpture

where the bent-bow bridge shoots arrows
                    at the sky.

I know the city is deaf
                    and cannot hear
the insolent whistling of a new lover,

nor the queer footfall of an iron bird
which strides toward it
with the strength of a migration.

19
A famished man

I savour the smallest morsels;

a pale blue star at the bottom of a pond,

a rocking headlight swarming with locusts,

the sad mime of the juggler's curve,
an orange left to die on the empty stage,

whatever overflows the fences,

whatever escapes the prim snipping
                    of the gardeners

to bend in ripeness
over the granite snow.

20
The islands are black spears.

The summer green is all in blossom
              up the mountain slope,

I puzzle out

the blunt perspectives of the forest,
the shifting levels
          of the open wood.
The faithful one, the hunter, senses my return.

He sees me walk in circles

as a sign of repossession

I stop and name the trees: the shagbark hickory,
the linden tree, pine and cedar, silver maple.
I stoop to pick up sticks,
          and biscuit-coloured stones,
and stones that glint with mica chips.

I catch the smell of soaking earth,
a metal in my throat.

I recognize the patterned zebra stripes of sumacs.

I fill and find at will.

A klaxon pheasant cry I cross with tauric blood.

I lie about and watch.

I crunch along the road to wake
the gold Mantegnas dozing in the rocks.

21

Sharon,
as you run ahead in this familiar wood,
I have no sudden intuition about the acorn's heart.
Did you know the conundrum of the oaks
was used as a magic by Druids?

I know this has no meaning for an eight year old.

Even so I feel its directions catching in your throat
like laughter, its solemn
nonsense spin my command
to the highest smallest branches.

You may try as I have done to lose yourself
in the orchards of the South.
It seems so desirable.

But there will always be a sympathy
as obscure in its origins as the quality of your colouring
which runs through the wood like a woven thread;
the sympathy which brings me back to these
gently sloping terraces.

What can I say?

For some there is the South, a sweet globe of fruit,
and for others, there is the dry
pointed riddle of the acorn.

22

Each year a new ring springs up around the city.

Look how fast we are growing,
chants the old chorus.

But it is not we who are growing,

It is the city,
dragging us along in the wake
of its transactions.

In this kind of growth we are less than a cipher.

It is time to unmask a tyrant,

I mean the clown who has us all by the hand
                              as if we were children.

We have come to speak nothing but its
crude slang of action.

Let us hear the sound of our own voices again.

Let us speak the dignified language of man.

Let us bring back from a bitter exile,
the colours of our exaltation.

23

I am almost asleep
with your poems on my chest,

Apollinaire

I am almost asleep,
but I feel a transfusion of fine little letters
dripping slantwise into my side.

Section Five

— Mexico

the road is straight is straight
sometimes enveloped in thighs of land
shoulders across its way
flats of brush and cactus stone and stunted trees
later fresh green splashes of maguey

is straight is planned
mountains faked by contours fail and disappear
then at last the ocean eased inside
a broken pot of shore
syrupy distasteful bilious with silver
gloating with stillness

Mountain teeth, tips of anemious rippled stone,
a glacier of white cloud settled into the tilting passages:

Are you there, Li?

Are you there in the mists, Li Po?

If I ring your two-change name against the massive greys will you
answer?
On this day and in this location can you see how it is with us humans?

There are greens about me here, and the pressure of the soft gloom,
animals in the rising fields.
                    Men I shall never see
stand in the doorways of their huts like true sentinels of life.
There are chimneys behind me rolling up the first balls of pale smoke.
A high plateau above, ceaselessly swept with tears of anemia,
before me, and always in my mind is the shape of peninsulas
as insistent as a black mirror.

The empty truck, traumatically still;
a score of men loosely grouped beneath a tree.
                    The stillness is the echo of an explosion!

I find the burlap square in the centre of the road
and I know that beneath it there is a dead child.

Is this what you meant by "waves," Li Po?

most of us welcome machines that make steady granular noises
or roaring ingest the air on ocean voyages or at the back of
                          darkened motels
the drains that slip our nightly messages bring stillness up and sleep
like the bursting out of flowers. . .

here I am awake and locked inside a brown and white colonial set
my isolation is a must of blue policemen (the rifleman I never was)
the wind a tower placing tokens on my eyes the coolness close
                        to violence
in its intervention. . .

and

I've finally met a clever Mexican ironist
a Toronto educated orthodontist
        as his wife was too
you (he laughed) Canadians are funny
funny yes and desperate said I
AND YOU SHOULD BE TOO

        we both fell bleeding onto the heap
        the fate of all
        good planners in sadness

        2
        a winter evening
nineteen forty-five the bus at rest
emptied of its bottled life bombarded
by a day and night of travelling
old curves catching up like boomerangs
pot-holes from the road outside Victoria

how I loved this place! the feeling of some brown accelerator
locked to the floor fed by the movements of blood
the smell of dryness chemical-natural-seminal
the sky with its
hypo of blue
pitiful palms like the musty dresses in a museum
dresses curving the streets in steady migrations

and the "Dali" character
who gave us a home
Italo d'Andrea dressed
in his purple turtleneck
and bowler hat or in his
purple silk-lined cape
there too
was blond and swollen Betty
Carmen from Santa Barbara made motherly
by her hard experience
Ron the gentle fugitive from justice
Henry horse-faced poet
from Amsterdam I was
the innocent one the straightman
I paid the rent

and there was a parrot who sang soprano
and who'd cry PAPA YO TENGO FRIO
when the clear black shade
started climbing in his cage

and the pair of medical students who probed
our minor infections like comic gardeners

joven!
si!
> *joven*
> > *joven*
> > > *joven*

and

> I haven't forgotten the night you clawed me
> down the back
> screaming hysterical too much spitting
> too much burning contact unregenerate noise
> gonorrhoea in the flabby
> singing faces children hustlers
> limbless bodies
> grinning turtles
> moving in your wake

ah the horror of it all

did you know that in nineteen forty-five almost all the city buses had holes
       in their mufflers and
did you know that in that year several teachers were killed in the great
       crusade against ANALFABETISMO
did you know that just behind the Zocalo there was a revolutionary circle
pledged to the immediate overthrow of the Guatemalan government
did you know that I read the name of Igor Gouzenko on the second page of
       the Grafica Noticias
and I knew in terrible loss that PEACE was a word for children to play with
       a lullaby

3

joven joven

       things have changed
       the gap remains the same
however

dust remembers water and its dense authority
glyph reshapes the pot the bug-eyed entity comes
streaming rain across the tortured evenings almost
unrecognized by lovers almost unchecked
by the clay-faced police
the city's lost momentum is notably our gain
the parked volcanoes shine as dully as a tourist brochure
the frantic cars decelerate with speed
yoked to a full-length portrait of Malinche

Marianna Yampolsky

You
haven't changed, Marianna,
buying glasses (tumblers) in a non-profit store.
I bet it's
a surprise for some chronic invalid
paralysed by the demands of his art.

I should have reminded you—
to draw
we once went up the mountains together,
the vultures would fly no higher.
You were
— so quick on your feet, so businesslike,
I soon forgot my breathlessness and my battering heart,
and the drawings you did.
That day I saw
that a golden snakeskin was really the winter valleys below;
for you
the jagged erosions were moral, this was your faith.

Details are still so clear:
the evening wind,
the bus arriving late stuffed with whiteness,
and like a primitive panel, a face in every window.

I can remember
passing you twice on a stairway,
as usual you talked of thrift and arrangements
and mercifully never looked at my eyes.
How I
envied you then your intactness,
even your name which was you in a triptych of sound,
Yampolsky,
fruit, roundness, and finish—
what wouldn't I have given
then for just one of those perfections.

Mexico—Siqueiros, Rivera 1945

Ambiente Particular

the first time
I saw the volcanoes I
was walking away
from the last bus stop
in the Lomas de Chapultepec
nothing prepared me for
their position in the sky
such mythic structures
on and of the land

the Mexican nation also
appeared as a volcano
an upthrust of people
its peak above the level
and distant strata of abstract ideas
its reality a fact even
in the blackouts of power
the dust storms of a largely
organic evolution

a claiming and unfolding both
backward and forward

no hay mas ruta que la nuestra he wrote
dictating our future with
that terrible drive of his. . .
           in the Preparitorio
singing likenesses striding down
and out through the past
chanting pallbearers planting
the martyr's seed of tomorrow's world
mystical workers heroic overtones
of comradeship and vigour

later it's the liberty cap
* *Nueva Democracia*
triple fists of dogma
breaking the chains

triple threats of ducco
         and
closed inside a bourgeois home
Cuauhtemoc Against the Myth

it's true he was intensely pale
the nostrils in his pictures were
no exaggeration

Sanchez bitterly—
he thinks he'll live forever
he might his grandmother
died at 112

historical rectitude means opting
for eternity means constant striving
after progress questionable labours

the proletarian clanking of the streetcar
heading for the Zocalo
catching sight of the Bellas Artes
feeling his presence
knowing he was there

*This mural was painted with pyroxylin over cellotex covered with cotton cloth. Modern tools and an active composition was again applied.

the courtyard of the National Palace
a mirror for the vanished
solar gods of both cultures
the dangerous chill in the soldier's urinal
in the shack on the roof
running our little pounce wheels down
the black veins of the "cartoons"

a season passed
with our backs to the light
facing the fresh white plaster
our elbows on the balustrade
no word from the maestro
ailing it seems

ten feet off the ground
placing a chair under Rivera's settling backside
bulging blue serge suit with
white thalidomide hands

watching the two together
refining an editorial
quiet and deferential
abdicating in the rarest sense
Trotsky's body between them
the nascent body of a Mexico both
more and less than they'd bargained for

note on Siqueiros revolution like form should
                            be spiritually biodegradeable

note on Rivera   in the evening under a single cup of
                            light embossing indenting the
                            forms hour after hour more like
                            a meditation than a gathering
                            synthesis

THE MESA MEXICO

Churches are candelabra
On the golden tableland;
Branches of jewels,
      a setting for the cool fat tile
            that quenches
As the new grass is an emerald oasis
In the bluish flame
        of day.

Water is currency;
Clear liquid silver,
A savage tease
      for the cracked rooting tongues
           weaned from the rain.
Shadows are obsidian, and the wind
A sickness, climbing up with feather claws.
          The sun

Rages in its closeness
To the shining domes.
Neither tropic nor arctic,
      the glacial mesa refuses to inflict
         its stinging secret
Into the moist flesh of men. The rattle
Of rocks and the queer dry stealth
         of lizards

Are its only clues.
Stars are needles
In a black pincushion.
      Goatherds are conspirators against
        the chill knives
Of midnight, Riflemen guard the sleepers
From a scorpion dropped into
         their dreams.

The leopard blood
Of centuries, the curse,
Corrupts the timbre
        of the grandest bells. The hills
                of grooved
And dominating gold engulf the bulls,
Marauding birds, and desiccated walls, in
                primal claim.

Start here —
With the taste of dryness,
                    hyena-spotted walls,
With a motto caught between bulging urns,
With cinder domes on stiff octagonals.
Start with freshness,
                    with the young girls
Frisking in the portales.
Start with the pigeons hauling up their buckets of light
To the ailing Parroquia.
Start with the Street of the Little Cradle,
Here was born Ignacio Allende,
                                colonial gentleman,
And martyr.
Start with the gradual slope of mourning.
Start with a
Fitted-in pygmy, whiter-than-stillborn statue.
Start with the barking of the dogs,
With flowers,
With words.

WITH THE SPRING

With the Spring I realize my fatigue
With the bare brown particolare hills
Behind the town. Not even a poet
Can face an absolute day after day,
Or find replenishment in basic form
And some enigmatic scratchings.
Each time the sun agrees to dissolve
The hills in a blue smoke they return.
The moon, trapped in a mirror of its
Winter estate is reminded of its nothingness.
I learn to like the Baroque at this time.
Strips of homely colours, and the liquid
Tiles of the town are scaled to harmonize
With the vagrant cycles of men.
Spring is no time for the fashion of the
Steel monument! And how can I praise
Things that are so still when growth
Is the word singing and turning
In the marrow like a leaf. I belong
In the valleys, in the company of the
Bougainvilia which is all hearts, with
Opalescent jellyfish sunk in the troughs
Of the bogus sea, the eucalyptus and
The fat pepper trees, and the pulsing
Mauve lamps of the jacarandas. I belong
To the anonymous coal green glitter and vine,
And to the sabal palms contained
Like giraffes in the white of the sky.

No.1

Set like a stone
In this bell jar summer town
Where the clock is officially stopped,
And the crusted bells
Can bark and hammer the days
Of the blessed saints in numbers—
I lie like a lizard,
Awaiting the loss of its tail,
Expecting my blood to thicken
To honey sap in a matter of days,
And the walls to proffer
The roots of words.

Hidden away
In a loft of inaccessible land,
Where the sun falls brighter than snow at
Twelve, I erase the
Sight of the muscular skylines
Sprouting a mile below
And the leapfrogging signs
That lead to a shabby neglect by
The whistling railroad track. I feel
The beard of my nonconformity
Wither like chaff in the midst
Of a green rebirth.

Fast and soft
As moss in my tile cool eye on the street,
I spin to a stop with the world at four
As familiar noises blur and climb
In the vertical heat.
I have only to lift my head
To watch my heroes pass
To choose in sight of the
Bloody poles of their life, the man with
The lion's eyes, and the woman,
Beggar and bird, with a child pressed close
To her sun black skin.

Monk and mate
In this cloistered house on the fly,
I work by day, my purple words on a
Narrow shelf of metrical light,
While the sun comes down in a storm on
The roof, and the sky is a horn
Of electric blue. I awake
In the cool and hilly nights
To make the most extravagant sign
Of luck on the one at my side.
For already the follower moves
In the valleys below.

No. 2
The Women

They came down from the hills,
The ones that made me think of blackberries.
Las zarzamoras sounds more beautiful.
The English word is plural, and like fruit.
It has the quality of eyes.
Las zarzamoras is more the dusky indigo
Shawls that swaddle them in jug shapes
On the blinding street.

With a look of the new-born,
They watch the tourists pass in colours
Matched against a silver skin. They squat
A perfect attendance on the more exuberant life
That spreads about them in that incredible way.
Glowing cones of oranges, oranges in hills,
Green limes, and onions live like teeth in
Their slippery skins, the uncompromisingly red
Fists of the peppers. And eggplant, shiny and
As black as wine that should be
Calabaza de Castilla.

No. 3
THE WALLS

The exquisite walls of San Miguel are for all—
For the rich man living high on the hill,
For the woman in the Carcel de Mujeres
Held on a serious charge,
For the jailer with his one white eye;
For the baby, as small as a monkey,
That passes by bound in a sagging rebozo—
Not completely unlucky, its helpless eyes
Parade the flaking splendor of the walls,
Black life on the dried flowers.

No.4
VIEW FROM A WINDOW

The tenderness so hard to swallow
is partly the two flies settled in her hair.
Her mouth opens to the soothing air,
drool scabs curving down from its edges.

And her brother whom she holds shyly for me to admire...
the mess of mucous and the clinging feeding flies...
awake, a toxic film covers his eyes
shifting mechanically in patterns of escape.

Across the steeply climbing flat-faced street
at the six vertical ochre strips
her older sisters, short skirts flaring from the hips,
emerge and blow away buoyant as wasps.

Beauty complicates the average squalor,
carries the unpredictable like fallout
into the brutal levels, burns about
the ruin and the green vine with its yearning.

She hangs around; she says she's eight.
Her name is tuned for ceremonial complaint;
mine is, that dozy flies can travel here without restraint
in the gentlest of hatchures.

MOUNTAIN TOWN

Arms at my side like some inadequate sign,
I lie awake in a dark room in an alien country.
While plates of frost slide past my face, and needles
cluster in the crêpe-like air, my friend who has made
his adjustment, urinates into a bucket with a thunderous ring.

I must impress myself with certain things;
the honesty of mountain people, the lightheartedness
of a people never conquered by arms — and yet
the monster of the mines lies dead beneath their homes,
its scattered mouths decaying in a final spittle of stones.

Into this piled-up town beneath astringent stars
what did we bring with us that is simple and hopeful —
into this confusion of times? Breadcrumbs for the blister
of the floor, bottles crowding off the ebbing surfaces,
memories of love, perhaps the gentle trauma of our intrusion.

A jukebox rumbles out a tune, the singer
holds her sex against my abstract form. We are the angels
of ironic movement, she and I. Our pleasures
are more permanent than the mountains here whose marrows
fired in a day form quickly into sediments of tragic angularity.

I lie awake until the blackness burns to filaments
of tired red. A horse sparks up the cobblestones.
A voice speaks cleanly from the stage of cold beyond.
No spout of sunlight ever entered to my bed, but stealthily
an orange cat comes snaking through the door in search of food.

Elbowing its neighbours,
San Felipe dozes in the sun,
A mask of senility,
A pink face gone askew
                        and
Spotted
Down the shade across
The way, black wrapped women
Wait like birds asleep
Among their jars.
It was here,
                just before noon,
The Minotaur appeared lost or
Caught off guard, skittering
As if the cobblestones were coals.
Everybody
            stopped to stare.
Everyone, that is,
Except the blind man who sat,
And smiled up at the roof tops,
His long hands posing questions.
Down
The centre of the street it came,
Horns in its hands,
Unsettled perhaps by the silence
Of the people, muscles tensing
On its narrow hips, the purple
Seeds of its virility
Swinging as it moved.
                        Later
No one could explain
The crazy angle of its head
                or say
Whether the expression in its'
Eye was one of terror or of a
Terrible moist hunger

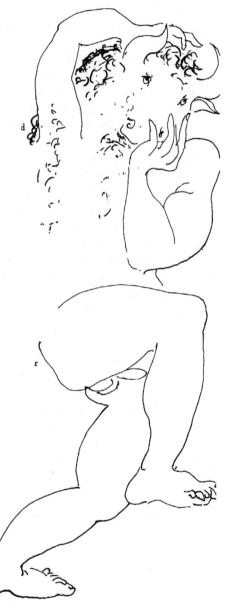

                    And
When
It veered and vanished
Round an angle in the street,
No one spoke
                              until
The parrot squawked, that hangs
Outside the entrance to
The butcher's shop.

D.G.

Too many Anglican chants
Have come between you and the
Natural business of song.
Still I admire you
For taking up the guitar,
And with a teacher who
Insists that you sing!
So let's have the one about El Raton —
       On the twenty-sixth of September I felt
a great emotion —
       Ole!

Famous, as he
Fiddles at his toys,
Don Francisco, the piñata maker,
Forms a green parrot
Round the belly of a pot,
And a perch of flowers cut
From his precise imagination.
Red and white, and
Blue and white balloons
Of tissue paper stripe the
Blackness in his shop.
At eighty-nine
He talks a quick deaf language
Of his own, and to emphasize,
He'll dart a finger at
The stars and bright plump birds
That wheel like pagan suns about
His calendar of joy.

KISSING NATALIA

Invention begs from door to door in the indescribable darkness,
a chorus of animals like canned laughter. I had it planned,
drunk though I was, to drive you to the edge of the town
and when you said 'thank you' as you always did, I was going to kiss you

This was the plan and in the calm of decision I got you in,
passed houses drawn up like fanatical serfs, my thin excuse
trailing lifelessly after us like a rodent tail. (The general's
coming, boys, and his aide-de-camp and faceless mariachis from the 'gatos'.)

The engine slowed as my heart rose, your profile, dumb in the light,
came to the edge of town, looked off to stepping stones
which glowed in the shallows, to total darkness, and Lord knows where.
You said, "thank you," and so I put my hand there and kissed you.

Were you scared? It must have come like a moon pie in the face,
and unprepared for an instant, the trembling ring of your lips
held me as a lover. The place reeked of the chemistry of rivers
I remember now, and your mouth left the slightest aftertaste of earth.

The young boy, Javier
Is so tired he doesn't feel the flies crawling,
His head rolling like a moon with fatigue.
Last night he fell asleep half under a car;
The night before with his head on a shelf.
But still he manages to protest when
His mother tells him softly, "Go to bed."
"Like a borracho," I say.
"Igualmente," she answers without a smile.
She remembers his father
Who came over the wall like a thief
At three o'clock in the morning.

MANZANILLO

And it didn't clear
Even though the fish-man said it would,
But who should be responsible, especially here
In this slightly tame 'Purgatorio',
Where the weather forces frames of conduct;
Rainy slicks where pelicans accelerate
Their day-consuming quest for fish,
                    and rays as big as table-tops
Come calmly nuzzling up the sand.
                        Most unusual you say....
Should we the bathers point out such mistakes,
Warn the warrior scorpion of our greater sting,
The spider and the serpent
                            of our ever increasing claims,
The slender spout-shaped birds
Who stand in stillness
Making sure appraisal of the foreign thing?

All day the grey Pacific combers
Have rolled toward the beach,
                        met opposition,
Towered green-glass up, and thunderously collapsed.

The empty freighter, a fixture of this place,
Leans against the sky,
Its function needling and clear beside the furry hill.
Starts swinging now with hour-hand deliberateness
About the twanging anchor chain.
What motion and relapse;
                        the festering black.
The slanting curtain-squalls, the vertical hesitations
Sucking up the birds like gutted leaves.

Could this be Aristotle's, 'energy working toward a goal',
Or Tlaloc avenging himself
                         by snuffing out the last volcano,
Then vengefully pelting flat
Its glittering pedestal of fields?
Neighbour! Fellow wanderer!

                         What exactly do you see here
Now that the northern fortress towns
                         are no longer under siege,

The last frontier dissolved,
Turning you upon yourself with all the despair
Of a jilted lover?
                    Are you liege to motion
Laving round the half-intended port?
Is it heat you want to coil itself about
Your cold and stiffening extremities,
                         a warmed retort where you may lie
Inert unquestioningly alive, perfectly suspended?
Do you claim sanctuary of your oldest enemy
Or recess from some personal vision of murder?

The window rattles
I remember that my first impression of the Pacific
Was of a cave of bats; essence versus the erotic,
Versus the thrusts and giant exhausted fronds
Of the palm jungles,
                         essence diffused
In the savagely living, forever ripe,
In seductive intransigence, obscene stillnesses,
In opulence compelling and almost now a dream
                              to that fierce incorporate
Whose present crisis is dominion:

To avoid oppression
Let us try to name this kingandqueen,
For it is time we admitted its existence.
The Egyptians had the knack to name the abstract,
To give progression to dynasty,
Lasting mystery to the intolerable idea.
The gift came easily
When you consider the frigid remove of those
                                        first seen stars

The pressure of signs,
The seasonal sentence gathering in the watersheds
But what genius to have invented the sceptre,
As curious a wedge as has ever been! And gold!

Give us equal genius
Or wit or humility or art to break the hold
Of these twin-sick old and fabulous expedients.

COLONIA

I

It starts with a stream;
Starts as it should start
                with humans,
Moving in single file.
And for this a path is cut,
Clearings made and fires lit
On the sheltering
Slope of the hill.
The lizards, frightened,
Slip from their ancient rocks,
And the rabble birds rise
In patterns of dark and light crosses,
Blinking interrogation
Over the chosen spot.

It starts
As it has often started
With slaves,
With bonds loosened, and
The confident sentries half asleep.
With sturdy beams, and a plan
                that calls
For a church,
A cloister for the monks,
Three great houses and
A drill square. . .
It starts with
Half an acre of gardens;
Someone slaughtered
By the great dogs,
The mind in its frigid art
Counting intentions
One. two. . .

II

And as it happens
The stories are true
              about the silver.
And the 'Europe' town takes shape
Just as it had been planned.
Stone is quarried
And hauled into place.
With its walls up and buttressed
The church looks for a long moment
Like a guildhall or a huge
Granary. But then
Come the tall diminishing crowns,
And the lace,
And the dome.

A slave is found
Who is clever with wood.
And another, a talented moulder,
Is given a dozen men
And told to hurry it up.
And sometime later
He is shown a book
By an old Franciscan (in his cups).
And the houses go up
With heavy Italian frills
              exactly like Spain.
And the town is linked
With other more prosperous towns.
The crowns are fitted with bells,
And the dome
Begins its miraculous work of symbols,
Lance, sponge, cross,
Thorn, nails. . .

III.

But in spite of this. . .
The sword and the brand;
            in spite of
The rigid apocalypse of plunging horses;
The perfect drop squeezed
From the artistic hand of charity;
The bells reminding, reminding
The voices intoning —
At birth —
Droning over the shallow graves.
In spite of the towers
Boxing the morning sun,
In spite of the word,
The work. . .

The peasant begins
To live by his wits,
To live as he has always lived.
The women, to move about like native birds;
The children, to gnaw
With strong white teeth
On the sugar cane;
The men to steal,
            to kill,
To salt the earth with
The only passion there is —
The passion to live, to survive.
The sun to prepare its massacres
With lips, with eyes, with skin;
The smell of dung,
With death on death
As it has
Always done.

WOMAN SELLING PRICKLY PEARS

She deals in
Rich cosmetic spots on piny leaves;
Deftly splits, peels
                      and portions out
With grave appreciation —

Glow of red, rot of heavy doors,
*   intaglio of green.*

Her customers, first two, then three,
Stand or sit in ritual isolation—
                      red on red —
Each in their heraldic role of husband,
Woman, boy, etcetera. . .
Rigid peasant figuration.

*   Crusty pink and purple of the pears.*
Satisfaction understood,
No opinions offered as she husks
The dusty fruit.

*   Naples-red, sienna,*
*   Red digesting into lime.*
Onion white,
*   low relief of darkened skin.*

View Through My Window
At The Brooks' House San Miguel

saguaro phallics straight as bars stripe
the light with tall high humour
the hills a sleeping animal
trees are probing insects fenceposts —
stitches in a doctor's accidental line
no paths an old man with a stick comes
out of nowhere goes where he feels
a schoolboy stumbles blinded by his comic book
goats sometimes appear — or do they?

yes like sleeping animals the hills — lion—gold
and high on top the Three Cross trick —
etched and distant tiny and despairing

HIDALGO AND ALLENDE

if this 'hero' pair could ask
who were Nova Hanni
Reva Carmen?
I knew and
they knew me too
what was the Alhondiga?

robbery on the road
land the colour compliment of sky
Guanajuato - rubble heap of gems
tunnels church pikes drovings
silver feeding red...and
lately Don Quixote

mobs as mobs should be
but then O Mexico
the fortress wins
the weight of Freedom slows them
cuts off their heads

and a lesser two
skulls on rotting poles
names?...who knows

* *Delores Hidalgo and Ignacio Allende were leaders of an explosive
Independence movement at the beginning of the 19th century. When the
movement failed they were executed, their heads were cut off and with the
heads of two others were placed on high poles outside the Alhondiga (a
fortress-like grain storage building in Guanajuato).*

Four Illuminations

I On Thinking. . .

Because of choice. . I must.
Mozart bore obsequities instead
                            of nagging,
But then his world was cut in three
And all the worms confined
To one section.
            Pompous noblemen, insufferable clerics,
Settled in a switching pergola of stars.
Different rules? Not quite.
Freedom is acceptance of the rules. . .
But not quite.

Then silk can come from sows,
And this a miracle of miracles,

The rule that we observe so
                            righteously
Is Plundering Benevolently Curbed. . .
But not quite.
                And from this, strangely, comes
Asymmetry of stars and verse,
Constellations hinting death, and
Strength of animals. . .
                            incredible, the Scorpion,
            alive,
Gigantic, in the taut imagination.

And this is gain by being robbed.

And this the old dichotomy
                            of worlds;
Its aging mask of work and love, of ugliness
And art; the paradox I love, the tease of thought
As natural as breathing. . .
                but not quite.

Ovid, city-spoilt presumptious,
Prophecies his own unchanging fame:
"Neither Jove's rage nor fire. . ." he begins.
          But only those who loved him
Caught the whisper of his death.
"Enclosed my latest poems,
                    one a catalogue
Of Black Sea fish. And did you speak
Of matters to our friend?"
                    he writes towards
The end.
Ovid never understood
                    the relevance of words,
                    the passionate imbalance,
The passion underlying passion.

(Pound on Eliot: Poetry betrayed!
Renoir on Picasso: "Take away that filth.")

Having touched the element
The poet leaves his drillholes
                    in a vast alluvium,
Ruined landscape.
                    sieved and sinking down
To fertilize.
Having died the living poet's proxy rides
The shifting crest,
                    the underlying passion,
          sea alluvion of life.

Ovid's OVID,
          demon equilibrist.

I can always justify contradiction
By saying that art knows nothing
       of its dialectic
If I settle in a hillside town
And not along the sea,
      I say
It is because some practical solution
Had to be found.

Location dreamed about
Is often an early image of the self.
The still water,
Nothing else but the child sweetened
       by its first loves
The colour or the quality of light,
Some of this intensity expressed in the
Accepted visual terms.

There are pools in 'della Francesca'
To show what I mean.
      And
      "La Familia al Lado de la Mar"
By Picasso is a perfect picture of a
Young man who is about to contradict himself.

Consistency, integrity,
      call it what you want,
Is a matter of feeling,
Of feeling at the roots.
It is by contradiction that we first
      discover its symbol.

To end these familiar epics
   we must all agree
To mothball the fortressed cell of One,
To stitch the hero, still brandishing an oar,
On strips of formally tempestuous green.

Unusual methods are usual.
   In another day
Carpaccio slew the Dragon
   with some beautiful notes on the weather;
And the Master of Aix. . .

But this is more in the nature of plastic prophecy.

   Probably
The classic example of method
Was when several merchants,
   acting together as a republic,
Married the sea.
   And the Republic consisted of:
Lights, vistas, pageants, architecture, splendours,
And some painfully beautiful boats.

The marriage lasted,

And agreeable persons are likely to say
That the sea was the luckiest.

A Walk

It's not too bad
To think of a man
Beating his wife with a stick,
But the reality is something else again:
The vicious swish,
The involuntary cry of pain —
Once, twice, thrice
       A final almost unbearable swang.
It made you cry.
It taught me with a shock
That truth lies just behind the door
       waiting to ambush,
That even in the stilled levels
Of Europe's past
       there grows the flaw
That behind the Chirico tower
The boar is counting on another
       clock-struck victim.
And this relates to all that we had seen;
A tender quilted sky,
The smooth bark that you remarked upon,
The lncongruity
       which made us laugh
Of some sharp American slogan
Pasted up along the ghostly flats.

Like ants—
                    lugging their fantastic loads,
Passing each other without a sign
On the whitened footpaths — females, broad
And tropically bright, hungry-looking males
Plodding by the paper-brown fences
Of the corn stalks, eyes popping from
                              the strain.
Not as yet, the date of their liberation
The mystic separation from the animal,
The glass terrain, the flat blue mirrors
                    of the sky.

Look freshly at the fixed convention
Of the hills, the old volcano grown
Stale issuing its daily postcards.
Shrug the vicious demons riding pic-o-back
Pulling at your heads with slack
                    sadistic helplessness.
Throw them to the ground.
Look round about you with a fresh eye.
You, child, serving the sleek indolent cattle,
You, washing, washing, always on your knees,
You, wrapped up from the naked sun
                              like an Arab
See how the mountain Zinantecatl finds
Turbulence in the upper air, plumes snow
From its steep windward bevel.

Grand and obdurate it moves against the elements.

And on certain precious days seems only
To stand still girdled by the soft
Opulent shadow of the timber line.

On Cities....

If not conquerors
then why not a culture hero?
Nezualcoyotl, Pachacuti (who was both),
sacred urbanists from the green apices of the continents
from the white lipped cordillera of Peru.
                    Of Tenochtitlan
Bernal Diaz de Castillo says, "'Like a dream . . . the enchantment
                    they tell us of in legend.'"
                    (This sort of talk from Cortez' men!)
Again,
          Cortez: "More beautiful even than Seville!"
                                        And yet
how completely they destroyed it all
as if the world could tolerate nothing but the European imagination;
and so in Europe's way the cities grew on other cities—
blue and grey, brick and sullen spots
                              in the
pitiless sunlight of America.
About our present day pragmatic landscapes
certainly
          more than we can tell...
men change slowly (unenthusiastically)
but caught so closely in this greatest swell and stray of city growth
                    much has broken loose:

mercantile is loose in tropic, creature-love in spirit lamp,
sky facades —
                    bioptic magic.

. . . the purest stele or a shell of some impersonal kind of strata?

DAY OF THE POOR

Symbolically
The Day of the Poor
Is light-starved,
        A slithering sky,
Lozenge shaped
Watery clouds
Blobbing up from behind the scene.

        And the black spider
Which is the poor,
The char about the door,
        Awaiting the handout
Of two kilos of maize
To approximately one in four;
        And this is more
Than is usually done.

I should mention
        A dozen grackles
Swaying together like iron flowers.
        And the soccer players
Cantering about
With ironic detachment;

        Smoke culled
The shouting, rustling,
The muttered expectations
Blowing steeply up the flue,

Roaring through a mousehole
        Into emptiness,
Sailing mice-like
By the clean figure of Andromeda.
"Breaker of Men".

Barbara In San Miguel

her name was Barbara and
her high white horse came to the door
(right through the narrow house that is)
hooves clicking up the tiles eyes
smoky and unfocused — were there goats as well?

a group of eight of us or less
in the close dark space listening to
"Man and Superman" by Shaw
astronauts of life somewhere in the
landglow emptiness of Mexico's plateau

American of course woman on
the go she joined a Red Cross 'something'
was jeeped about the sun-fried streets
barbarously blond waving high at friends
one hand holding tight
one leg pitching from the side

life-blare in its void
syrup over the dam this
fleshing out with animals these
flashings from the homely punt of disasters

perhaps a visitor from space (from
space outside) could pluck her from thls
parched indifference timeless resignation
sweet intense and dry as fresco

that's what came
rich man from Alaska who marries
her in haste . . . then dies
Salmon Faith and ritual we thought
Inseminate wlth glitter
racking off that soaring blush helpless fermentation

Up Here When A Storm Breaks

Up here
When a storm breaks
(And it seldom does)
I act like an incompetent mariner,
Climb in a slow bulk
To the sealing off of windows and doors,
Cling miserably to the railings
While the sea boils below
Along the garden walls.

The static ground,
The upward growing town
Becomes a surfboard
Accelerating in the wind.
The hanging lamp travels distressingly,
The leaves from the lemon tree drop behind,
Are swirled away,
Small lights, twisted by the force
Of countless insensible gusts,

And the spirits
Which possess my seven rooms
Develop weaknesses as if to try me,
A terrible susceptibility to jets of cold
Which lays them out
As if they were Juliets — dead.
I must go about
Carrying sulky flames of encouragement,
Scurry round
My ship of ridiculous situations
(A suicide in every room),
My indefensible architecture of tombs.

And when, quite suddenly,
It blows away
This topsoil, torn from the sea,
It leaves me grateful,
Always shaken from the long watch;
Waking, incredulous of the blue
Which beams up, up like indirect lighting;
Lost in admiration
As the sun reheats
The pink stalagmites of the Parroquia
With a million midget flares.

My Hands For Sylvia

Much more than my eyes
my hands have become familiar with you;
through the twin valleys of my sensual palms
you slip, seize, wax cold and warm.
the serpent of my finger needs no other senses but its own.

My hands can tell more exactly
the beautiful thing that you are although they are dumb.
Have you noticed how they are constantly speaking to you
with small vibrating tongues?
The tension of touching you raises on them a velvet nap,
a friction of love.
O what have you not explained
to these ugliest of all appendages!

And in the aftermath
when limbs turn turtle into thc rippled sheet,
and light strikes gently to the brain,
the eyes, too practical for love, regain the lost role of explorer.
The hill outside they see
as if it were trembling in its own image,
as if reality had lapsed again to some limpid and more poetic state.

And hands at the end of their broken branches
lie freighted down like the fruits of an imminent harvest.

DELORES HIDALGO

The invisible town
The remote foothills
Await the new masters.
Past are the pyramids
              the priests in parrot robes,
The black business of the cross.

The spacious jardin
Bleached by the sun,
The plaza, cleanly swept
By the wind is left
              to dogs and the easy strays
Of the in-between.

The church descends
With a sweetness
Of numbers. It will survive.
Though its doorway is a socket
              it will grow in the eyes
Of the newcomers.

MAN OBSERVED — SAN MIGUEL

I owe you nothing
Having suffered the exigence of your anger
And felt (like something real)
The stage-smoke puff about
Your ineffectual exit.

Buckle on your belt.
Squint from the white centre of your rage.
Already the whimpering subsides
And the house, full of your generous commitment,
Warms
Forgives
Impels you back.

Your weakness, that of loving, is unusual
Affection leaves you paler than the rest,
Sharply taut, then weak,
As if some foreign drug were in your veins.
Nothing here explains you to yourself,
The virtue of passivity,
The bond,
The mindless langour of the feminine star.

But you are theirs
And through them you are inescapably known
In the close willing steps of your youngest girl,
In the fruitful body of the boy,
In the moving ceremonies
Of dressing up
And combing out the dark disquieting hair,

And most surely in the way
Your eldest leans against the door
Free, unfixed — because of you — innocently sexed.
Her eyes and smiles gratuitously merging
With the vast blue chemistry of December afternoons

SYLVIA AT THE ECHLINS IN SAN MIGUEL

tone-flat on an early
sun-filled window (Mexico no less) profiled in
that beige-white one-piece nightdress
Your hair's rich mass covers the eye so
only the nose leads out the mouth gives mood
does it press together with pleasures with satisfactions
does it constantly savour feelings words memories
tastes ideas...the dreamy flavours of Art
is there something in this growing light that
gives it such compactness eloquence of shape I
read with all my heart

MOON

In 1978 an Aztec stone weighing 20 tons and representing the moon goddess Coyolxauqui was discovered under the Zocalo in Mexico City

I must have walked over it once
a young man with a
nose like a sun-lipped chisel
busses with their sombre and chaotic loads
would have rattled it deeper into silence
streetcars entering stealthily
making their robot turns
winding the rails like string
round its non-existent aura

I don't want you to think that this moon has died
I want you to know that it has been discovered and
that it is solid and present, countering the black hole
myth has a core like a peach stone
illusion though not our food is totality —
face like a thousand mirrors

the President was having his lunch when
the digger banged its jaw (shark's teeth in the air)
the sun was riding out its contract with
the sort of dedication Mexicans expect
word got out that treasure had been found under
the Zocalo — Montezuma's loot to be exact
the population lurched at the thought of this reprieve
this dowry that was certainly theirs

the site was roped off just where the white
mass rose with what looked like a passion of
stylized feathers and severed limbs on its surface
archaeologists came and went and
reaching out like primitive athletes
grazed it here and there with
their billiard cues of the past

a tremor (though always of doubt) shook
the trade union masses
the unemployed students whose malice had spread
like the stale spots in a chocolate bar
blurred out their separate patches
the National Pawn Shop drew its blinds and raised
its rates in a careful gesture of mourning
the media people just stood about or angled their
photo-guns with obvious disrespect
occasional flash burns swallowed the yellowing light
flushed the grackles out
of their manicured trees like grapeshot

the second day — a firm communique
headlines shrank inflation dropped unnaturally
the President picked up his artfully folded
napkin with almost a tinge of sadness
the mystery (or treasure) was
the Moon-thing itself or Coyolxauqui
a woman needlessly torn apart by *SUN AND WAR* as
that new-born barbarian burst from his mother's
womb burning for justice and fratricide

that she was lovely comparatively guiltless and HIS mythical sister are
probable clues to this pure and unscheduled rebirth — her petrified sur-
vival

for the rest of the day the 'Palace' sentries
stared from their boxes oafish relaxed
resuming their headstrong rush
streams of glittering cars as
inexhaustible as water flushed
and deepened rectangular beds
the ant-lines of civil servants
the workers who tidied the Plaza the
blank-faced clusters who came and went
were almost hostile
the Moon they felt if it had to come down
to earth if it had to hide should
have chosen a burrow mercifully remote
favoured a crater in the taiga a mine shaft
deepened for nuclear disposal

business executives noiselessly rose
and sank in their frost-lit elevators
were sometimes seen to merge and divide behind
seascapes of river-thick glass bullet-proof doors
horizons of immaculate lettering
if they thought of it at all they thought of
the Moon in terms of gloss
the Moon-and-Art in terms of resale value
the Moon-as-Myth-and-Art as
part of a media spectacular like
something called 'the Past' —
a sales perversion a chemical facsimile

flexing its plantlike fixtures the
Plaza had joined its legacy of shifts its
chronic apostasies (under a tense blue sky
soaked in this native 'air' is how
I remember the place)
the city so huge it could hardly breathe humped
and spread and was temporally relieved
in the sagging shade of a tarpaulin
the great white stone (now bared to the waist)
was stillness itself detachment
indifference Form in the flood of
movement of anguish and luck of helplessness

the shift and swing of a crane was a first
unearthly step to its permanent home (the place
and prominence of setting were never in question)
determined to crate it with words art experts
(merging their settled domains) issued a
glossy catalogue a culture prospectus
dealing in pros and cons —
the site of the Moon-thing's turbulence
candle power versus formal putrescence...

prize-winning scholars brilliant professors
made cabinets for its leisure
theorems for its passion
manacles for its so-called proliferations

a student half awake I'd wait for my streetcar in the shade...on the moon
side of the street (as symbols Sun and Moon were hit or failure ratings —
failure like the spreading dew of dust on the squatters' roofs)

the President's Mercedes up from its underground garage
the President's profile climbing a slit in its landau top

the President taking one day at a time
like a man with a serious disease
sees the moon kicked up from
the glowing tip of the freeway
a curator of Aztec objects dreams of a 'Western'
moon that preserves itself that graces
the peak of a pyramid like a finial

and the Museum Director (pale and involved
as his name) unable to sleep and pacing
the linen whiteness of his room catches sight
of the moon incinerating itself in
the blackness over the Pedregal —
its organs its feathers its features its limbs
its captive race
its deathless personae
its furious and wonderful return

* *Huitzilopochtli was the Aztec god of sun and war*

Maya

in classical times
(the world supported
by the four Bacabs)
in the year that started
with I Imex O Pop
the priests are parading in
force in pectorals and
cloaks buccal masks
attended by rattles
and outsized trumpets dancers
disguised as alligators

incense flails its blue
experience faith is voided
from the white entrails
of the conches athletes
puke in fervid exhaustions
the artisans strain from their
pen in the fourth barrier
the Lance is held in
a false gold hand by a
personage infinitely noble

all the paths have been
beaten and redefined for the
fete of I Imex O Pop
vegetable headdresses close
on the cross-eyed boy who
lays his staves across
the calculations in an
angle of caution women
fussed and ecstatic in a
square outside the Square
merchants grooming their patron
Ek Chuah

there is no horn rubbing
louder than another danger
slaked to lengths in
the cooling lime rhythms
brass in intention
suicide is represented
the stele of weaving
the heretic unit of
leap year royalty by
rumours of jadeite the jungle
by its splits of birds
medicine by serpentine

beads as moist as cherries

the felly of the sun with its
three optical bands

One knows nothing but
The huge hot presence of the sun. One has
Childlike dreams of Morning Star and jade.
One sees arms extended in the sky,
White arms, faintly on a windy day.
One discovers straightness in the new grey road.
And one believes that Tlaloc stands
Behind the hills spilling the smaller clouds
From his fabulous head-dress.

Section Six

4 Flashbacks Metis Beach Lower St. Lawrence

I   Not Really a Place

not really a place in itself
just high rock and a tree in
the centre of a field
we called the "island"

the railway was something else
bossed by a proper Irish widow from
her shady beach house built
before the town discovered beaches
fifty miles of track three
recycled locomotives
wooden coaches windows slipped
by straps for easy spitting

shovels cached at the "island"
to think (I think) we dug
a trench in the railbed just
at the cross-ties' edge
covered ourselves with blankets
when we first felt the trembling

held each other down
as the sun went black
the search became reality

wind of heated metals
   grease
piston boxes grazing
slathering steam breathing
victims like a minotaur

NOTE: *We boys dared each other to lie as close to the railway tracks—when the train goes by.*

vertical fusion — fog and night
a masterful blackness
an Africa of weaving

a canoe with
a campstool in the middle
two of us paddling
one of us enthroned

the three-beat
circling beam of the lighthouse
carving a luminous block of
giant asbestos threads holding
us in suspension
one of us enthroned
two of us working like demons
gibbering Amazonian

at last a
grounding on stones
delirium subsiding a neutral
reality talking of substance
darkly admonishing

voices calling our names
the lights of a car
round with anxiety
yellow with fear

III   MR. KENNEDY — A MEMORY

Here comes the dwarf on his bandy legs,
Poling along with a stick as big as himself.
The birds fly up along his habitual path
And the sun avoids him crossing a yellow road.

Here comes the dwarf on his daily sashay,
His eyes as solemn as plums. Doesn't it give
You the creeps to know he pictures romance with
Every delectable girl that passes en route.

Here comes the dwarf from his special wood.
The children giggle and glance as he waddles
Their way. "Watch out for Billy Candy", they hiss,
And hope for one of his dangerous looks.

Here comes the dwarf on his regular trip.
The river bursts with an idiot grin as he
Catches his coat in the stile. They say he eats
Nothing but porridge, and carries a whip.

IV   MOISE PAQUETTE

at the edge of
        the Great Depression
                Moïse Paquette of

the baseball cap
        (the garage owner and
                district bootlegger)

joking it up with
        my father on the
                lost St. Lawrence (blue

strip facing the Arctic)
        while his cross-
                eyed boy of nine

(adopted they said)
        filled up the Marmon
                from a tall mesh-

wrapped cylinder of
        distilled cranberry juice
                "mornin Chas!"
                    yes

we knew the routine
        my mother defining
                her isolation my

father's face at play
        (at work?) like a
                Sun Mask wooden
                    houses

strung along the poor
                        powdery grass a
                                        chain of seaweed-

coloured rocks the sky a
                            soothing oblivion
                                            like silk

indulgent enormous
                        listening
                              as we did

Descend the country of the beach in a grand
Slide of rocks, jungled by the wasting sea,
Crevassed and sundered rusting in orange
Lichen. Rouse the kinder field of boulders,
Round with ripeness mortared in a curious
Microcosm of clay, shale, ends of sea-
Shells, hosting spiny urchins and warlike
Barnacles. Surprise the water at its
Ultimate recess across the freedom
Of the sand bar, pitted with breathing holes,
Rippled with the face of pools.
Chart the peripheral land from phallic light-
House to maiden spire, perhaps an arc of
Thirty miles. Arch to the rim of river.
Inspect the faint mirage of shore. Read in
The travelling sky treachery of the East
Wind. Focus the puppet ship.

More than anything else I came to watch
The ships always passing between lighthouse
And church spire. Lumber scows making the next
Wharf, ancient coastwise steamers bound for Bic
Or Anticosti, coal boats soiling the
Sky, tankers riding empty out to sea,
A liner briskly climbing the horizon.

I had almost forgotten the excitement —

Of the waiting presence of stones, of the
Cymbal sea noise, a lonely holiday
Of sound riding on the wind; and so much
More that has joined forever instinct and appearances.
The dramatis personae of my craggy
And sentimental stage—the earnest ships
Whose shapes remain, but whose names have dropped from
Memory one by one like ducks in a
Shooting gallery.

CHU YUAN (332-296 B.C.)

books falling down!
that stupid cat
making a place to sleep
an inaccessible hideaway

dig through the
monstrous clutter chasing
her off pick up
a book I'd forgotten
The White Pony

idiot cat racoon-like fur
bunched angrily over
her shoulders has
kicked out the words the One
I'd been waiting for —
poems of Chu almost
obscenely virtuous Chu

from the time of
Greece's disintegration
holdlng me by the throat
chanting me his troubles

granting me his exile

I Am One Who Sleeps In The Lap Of An Old Port

I am one who sleeps in the lap of an old port,
awakens to the sad cat cleaning of the waves,
shores up head with arm in the manner of Walt Whitman,
scrapes nail on toe to feel if it is really now.

Too familiar is the deaf-sight of the place;
peninsulas menacing like pineapples on a smooth plate
tonsils in a blackened throat, musical pudenda
to the oldest of the raving life surrogates.

Growing slightly sick of my extended day
I slant a string of words at prominent solemnities,
stretch to see them stop racked zig-zag in the picture light,
grow sharper and more lyrical than was intended.

Dreams can bring about a synthesis of time;
telescope to plausibility the passion of a dozen lives,
take and then deracinate the boy who seeks
hypnotic landscape rather than a fusion of the first felt.

I am one who sleeps in the lap of an old port
nourished by the claimless blizzards of its visitations,
half alive to forests of retorts and spines
and caissons rusting down the dangerous water drops.

YOUNG MANHOOD—
WOMAN IN A STORE ON MONTREAL'S GUY STREET

the store was a sweltering den of
body odour woman distress
when she finally realized my presence
she dealt with me blindly through
the thick luminous walls of what
must have been a raging fever
I felt a sexual awe for certain
"older" women like this one and
almost lost my head in those
sumptuous rancid emanations
I wanted to say something infinitely
kind and civil and I also wanted
to press my firm cool penis up
and into her centre drawing
the poisons away from that
fabulous-ordinary fever-shimmering goddess

MEETING IN PARIS
For John Glassco

God knows what another poet should look like.
When you came on with hands shaking
(after a taxi crash)
I saw nervousness and Englishness
and I
crossed arms against the body blow of meetings
after so much time alone.

Soon cognac froze
the sensitive word centres
so they came less jerkily
swelling up like a sleeper's heartbeat
then falling comatose.

"My book," I said, "my book". . .
knowing you found me unlettered —
the ceiling pressing down on us like a silk cloud.
Beardsley, and Tennyson (neither of whom I had read)
then an Edwardian magician—

I finally came up with Clare
and a belch of optimism
which smelt, of all things, like clover.

... and I wanted to warn you
      I saw God as a musician — your God
as an ugly albino in the midst of his sallow-faced men;
they wore smoked glasses to fend off his brightness
      and preached out the music of this phoney homeland.

To tell you this I had first
      to make you up from a river I'd seen,
a tree, a face with the true quality of rapt imagination.
You must stand up barefaced and ask, "Criminal One,
where are the bamboulas? How did the cask and calfskin sound,
and before the calfskin . . . original drums?"

My tribes have been ravished too,
      by Romans, Norsemen, men of the Cross, et al;
nothing much has been lost but the sound of the golden bells,
      but I have the gift and I can remember these.
      PEAL, is the first word in my vocabulary
or something so close to it that I am satisfied and at ease.

In the case of yourselves
      intentions are not so clear. . .
      the Mysteries of the new world. I tell you
to sing in the crowded dormitories or your spirit will coarsen;
under the tin roof at night, recall in detail, remember. . .
      suffer the ache of nostalgia under the blazing tin
or you will live like dogs — you and your generation.

The food will be bad
      so remember the taste of yam and mudfish.
Your imagination, useless on the Premises, will be
hounded down like an outlaw. You are the lambs to which
      progress is being brought; this old world
whose own progression rattles fatefully like a giant calabash.

As soon as you can
        you must read the ledgers of history
with good in the black column and bad in the red.
        You will notice that massacres still blow up like
        the dry winds of the spirit.

And when they have tamed you to the machines
        (and bauxite, manganese, gold, are rolling out)
You will find that earth has not always been so hospitable;
        there have been times of sickness and monstrous anomaly,
        and suns too small to be believed.

I see you coming to Accra
        with your pockets jingling
and a head as empty as your father's turned-down pot.
        The crooks will be waiting so treat them roughly,
and powerful men offering revenge and paradise on the blade
of a rusty sickle. Argue with these. Just as you are,
        dive into the smoking waters of politics.

As I said I have
        had to make you up from an instant
of flash-lit skin, a clearing, a plain from Mexico etc.
Your modesty though, and your imagination,
        these things are real . . . the striking look of your first poems
like handmade beads on a string, and the feel of them —
        wood, bone, shell, velvet, damask.

OSKAR KOKOSCHKA

I'm not sure really that I like his work; the colour stained,
the drawing straining in a hard scribble;
apple blossoms, lobster, a hanging grouse, flashes of disintegration
for which he preferred the medium of water-colour.

"A very considerable training." What did or do the Viennese
know about the art of painting? He knew and still knows
though now a septuagenarian surgeon (famous) between operations,
eyes overtopping, hallucination not of the common man.

But does anyone paint cities the way he does, many-positioned,
multifaceted? Could anyone but O.K. give to London that
                              quality of elation,
blow Amsterdam blue beneath the sea's level,
or show us a Lyon with the birds flapping in our faces?

"Part of the world's imagination," he might say of *Genoa Harbour*,
which is one of my favourites, and this is true of the *whole* painting;
ships aimed like missiles at the harbour's prognathy,
and the citadel (since destroyed) beneath a stationary cloud.

But what allowed him plum and mustard colour and that sweetish blue,
exotic overtones, to my taste, unpalatable.
Walls leap true like dragon teeth in the spate of execution,
a sculpture topples from the wings—Europe, and a fresh strain of polity.

As I approach St. Louis, Missouri,
The birthplace of T.S. Eliot and
Marianne Moore, I presume to
See this most poetic lady coming
      From the zoo, or seated
        Quietly in the park,
Finding the fragments she so
      Skillfully joins

Together. Does anyone say, "Over
There is Marianne Moore, the poet!"
I suppose they have you taped
One way or another
      As some ineffectual
        Old nobody; after all
Who else would sit in a park
      Or stand

In a zoo with the air of
A jade collector. Your perverse
Affair with the animals, the fish,
The birds and the beautiful
      Bits and pieces
        That become ugly
When joined into the monstrous
      Commotion of the whole,

Is a most ingenious and intelligent
Answer to an indissoluble problem
Posed by your refusal to travel further
Than an acquarium. Miss Moore,
      How can you live
        In Brooklyn? How does
That bird-like armour you wear repel
      The slugs and wallows

Of an outrageous romanticism?
And what does the tiger feel
As you disengage from the amethyst
And indigo dappled walk?
              Ennui, ennui, and
                      No food. Love
Is out of the question. Most likely
              He assayes the toughness

Of your beetle-black, straw hat
Thinking armour; and thinking danger
He eyes the flowers remembering
Delicious looking, oleander blossoms
              By what may
                  Have been a
River bank. I don't mean to
              Sound facetious.

Just how do you do it without
The tragic expedient of taking up arms?
How can you separate with the
Passionately dispassionate eye
              Of a camera,
                      Fragments which become
Poems of clear hard colour joined
              With strips of lead —

Mosaics of allusion to inhuman nature,
              And to your own
              Remarkable peace of mind.

Quebec — Revisited

I wasn't expecting it and I don't exaggerate
but some recent poems of yours have brought
me back to life turned me round and round
like a radar beam scanning
the soft blue tear-line of the mountains

I'm feeling your flexed components inside me again
a meal of candle-cracks textures tensions
longing that's poured its blood and waiting
into the mortified images of winter

someday soon your pressing songs may stretch and
sleep their night on a rockbank of stillnesses
stillness bearing the cuts of your fingernails
the ruts of parochial boredom your whips

your three profound conversions. . .
laughter helpless with reverence and fever
fasting with a bright incontinence

    2

once in 'sixty-four' going back or forth on
yearly migrations within your borders I came
on a barricade of white words painted on
dark-age country paving QUÉBEC LIBRE

my homelessness at that moment turned to yellow oil
the great neutrality in which I'd lived without
a single pact of communion turned its back
a word from the public cabal of language was now
worth more than childhood movies snoring genealogies

uneasy though I feel I wish you all success
your bishops in the past your "bishop" in the future
are more than a match for the spear-like arrow
(blue at either end) that fixed my morning dream
anchored tidal waves in simple contradiction

I can't forget you ever and how we both stole
sides of the same apple chewing it differently
living here "out west" with polygons instead of farms
wilderness in place of patriots cities
that are chrome and sealblack untouched flesh . . .
I'm turned to other confrontations sometimes

see you slickly as the railroad Chateau set
against a sweet undreamed Tiepolo sky
which must be something missing something else if
we are (fractured or together) turning this to peace

A Shopping List For English Canadians

Let us stir in the surface of the landlocked lake of yesterday's dessert.

Let us compromise the life appointment of the magistrates of
the vigilant tower.

Let us poison the moonlit style of the pimp of the turreted garages.

Let us hurdle the lust of the landladies of the self-made virtuosi.

Let us capture the wings of the tasseled bit of the charge of
the cereal cowboy.

Let us master the contours of the cattle skulls of the metropolitan police.

Let us crush the persistence of the paperweight of
the highly mortgaged factories.

Let us wrestle the morbid vagrancy of luck through the guillotine of
the neighbouring doorways.

Let us trap the sacred deterrent in its intricate breast-work of
office furniture.

Let us break to the crawl of the tremulous lights on the banks of the chasm.

Let us howl to the hollow flame of the windows of the beach cottages.

Let us close with the wrack of the fumbled wife in the razored arms of
the shutters.

NEW YORK, MYSELF AND ONE OTHER

1.

Needs no I or You
to hide us from itself, being largely sediment;
cliffs of anonymity and a few
exceptional peaks honestly lacking distinction.
Mountains are like this, huge and not huge
outweighing our need to implicate
our passionate loquaciousness. Lorca, go home!
Walt, stop flogging yourself
with that corny ceremony of calling!

2

Why can't you speak? (you know how I fear soliloquy)
Why should we have to move for entente?
Taxi drivers are taxi drivers, they take you places, they...
The woman in the No. 5 bus who cries, "I must have a ride
in that Zeppelin!" What should I do—
trail her like Breton, find out that madness exists?
The poets will meet on Wednesdays, Doomsdays, Thursday at 3
P.M.(the ballroom),
in Corso, in Ginsberg, in academic supermarkets, there, and there, in
underground committees, and in the most unessential lacunae;
            clocks, aborted beatitudes!

How did I know that those were negresses from Martinique?
Because of scale in their gestures, their musical intelligence.
How did I know that Puerto Ricans actually exist in the city?
I felt the dying of the magisterial— of tropical ideals.
How did I know that Harlem was Harlem?
I saw that the greensward was gone, that nothing would
                        grow in its place.
Why did I think Eilshemius belongs to the past?
Because the sky would preclude the gentle spoof of his dreaming.
How did I sense the fulfillment of women as women?
Because I felt their slack perversely, I was free to touch their
                        magnificent clothes.

3.

We've seen so much today
and yet so little impresses you (only the cry from the heart, your
                                tragic corner of complaint).
Don't you feel the city clapping back beneath your steps,
can't you invent its cilia or its yeasty embededness?
Isn't the name of a street indicative of something?
A Hundred and Tenth (I'll say it for you)
how disciplined it sounds, how cold but how slyly secretly involved—
                                  rings with rings.
A hundred and nine, a hundred and eight...
domes and corrugation, a feeling of brass.

Should we go forward, back
                       (I'm waiting)
should there be cities, poems, persuasions, artichokes of words?

My Winter Past

I owe nothing to winter
because it is not my way to be cold
or to be covered like furniture in a deserted house:
my father was flickering warmth;
feelings poached in the living white of my mother's passionate
isolation;
my brother's hands said what he had to say (and died without
saying).
I wore down the evenings with mirrors of flesh and wool.
I trampled a landscape of frozen hysteria,
cried out fear with my winter joy.
A child with needle in brain,
I armed myself with the physical sweat of kitchens and drugstores
and gravies and lightbulbs and dreams...

What was queer
was an all-deceptive peace:
midnights of burgeoning snow, charcoal cupboards of heat,
the actor's clap of the door — a knock on wood,
a single breaking wave in the family of stillnesses;
smoke behind the trees so pure so very far, tumescent, imperially weak.

> . . . Beneath a continental grey
> inside the brilliant tear of cold
> in the visceral voices of women
> in the fossil of the windows
> in the ragged nostalgia of sugar, of fever
> in the fruity dampness of wool
> in the licorice veins of my sensuality.

JOHN LYMAN

I

luxe calme et volupte
an option that now
seems slightly reduced
if preordained an image
refined in daylight
ripe civilities. . .

he took some pride
in the fact
that his feet were small
he laid out his palette
like a druggist which
his father was. . .

no Yankee cousins
Canadian foreigners in France
his solitary neighbour deep in
the spreading continent of art
was inaccessible
1907
the bourgeois summers rolled on
gathered unnatural sweetness
the art professors worked
at their blossoming charts
dabbed with classical measure
cut with magical vigour
a single
projection

II

I met him almost by chance
(my sexy aunt who worked on *The Star*
"of course I know an artist"
and she did)

in Montreal
                    I remember
the faintest echo of Cannes in
Senneville (a place he knew well)
a harbour much too muscular
for Marseilles-Toulon
a number of long straight streets
on the east side of the Mountain
which could have been France
'under a blizzard of flags'
a river flattened by farms
graceless table surplus serenity. . .

I still revere his icy
"Grier your fly is open"
an evening of tenuous depth integrity
there was even a "Legion d'Honneur"
and I was seventeen
and had painted my first real picture. . .
an authentic Arab a
Beothuk I wore his art
like a jellaba
tracked my innocence about

III

but what did I see
what do I really know
that isn't statistical
other-researched or second-hand
he was born in Biddeford Maine
(a link in the Connecticut connection)
at three his mother died

father Frederic Gold Lyman
unmated layman of success
spaceless architect of springboards
LYMAN'S DRUGS before my time

"even before the flattest
Quebec landscape I feel more. . ."
he wrote in his diary 1927
coming home to Montreal
ah the miserly stale
humanity of being "French"
the rootless monied sickness of "English"
ankle-deep in the good grey slush
we stood our ground
waited you could say flinched like
plants in the
clear enamels of cold
summers of tropical closeness

IV

1909
he found Matisse like
someone catching a stationary train
at the last moment
he and the Britisher, Matthew Smith,
were late comers
the convent converted to art
was in the hands of
Swedes and Germans
Europeans polished young rich
exclusive. . .

colour serenity beauty
values pushed to the limits of
taste and rationality
mind and senses in ecstatic proverbs
imperial configurations
Le Dejeuner   the table as altar
La Danse   esthetic vertigo

Grande Nature Morte aux Aubergines
sensation as myth
intelligence as colour
colour as transcendent order

riding the
top of the road
brutal flaying
but for
        PROTECTION
this world we've made
suburbs
blooming exhaustion
terrible trick of fate
        a place so decently lit
feel sensitive tonight feel sick
I howl for the future like a dog
emptiness and fuck
miracles and slack
        a place
        so decently lit
        so nothing
        &
        so perilous

Laddered for escape
>> the poet turns to wonder and perceive,
> Christbeard, naked for science,
>>>> loinclothed for God.

> The central character, the monster,
landed from his bark is scooping the
shadows for victims,
>> flushes medihorse
>>> and beautiful ghostcarnage.

Innocence, of course, he toucheth not,
> nor breaketh he the lamp so loath to light;
flowers poetical in fright
say bye to the mummy death.

> Women, special case, are quite
preoccupied with doves;
>> Madonna of the testicles and
>>>> Beatrice ofthespeechlessgrace.

The mythic sea is plate
> the human puzzle ready for the heap.

For The Painter Betty Goodwin

We chose because
we are chosen for this solitude, because
we choose to affirm its luxuries;
this opposition without counters,
without aims, these private revelations
for the public domain of feeling.

I knew your face and you knew mine
I think of lights in 'time'
installed without the proper connections, of buds
bewitched by the solid epochs of winter
which for you meant custom
and for me
the props of a ghostly metaphysic.

Our emotion has trapped us,
emotion for feelings which
made the intolerable pattern,
and yet we choose this manifest pain
rather than peace, rather than a soft release
and death in the public wish.

We can't and won't rebel.
Anguish-pleasure is a
time-tried combination, and we as mediums
are free of blame especially
if we mirror faithfully, vivaciously
or if we pose as
pilgrims on a difficult way.
I have to add how pared you've grown
how artful and aware, how well
you ride the slope of these imperatives.

met two hippie priests on the road   offered them place
     I in my car   they on foot
mouton hats sexless beards   overcoats of the after-war
     they sublime   I intent on the laws of driving
                 so where do you live
I inquisitive   they content   the sea immense like
  blue myopia itself   the sun conducting its burning
    off in the deafness of space
                the Island they say   the Island of course
then Boaz the forest primaeval   potlatch the morals of plenty
             SPEND TILL IT HURTS
    they informative   I like a plant in the rain
                they at peace
   unfolding the faith the poem of their day

1917

I was born in 1917 the year of

the ballet Parade

with costumes and curtain

by Picasso and

THE RUSSIAN REVOLUTION

what else happened

CENDRARS QUITS PARIS   SAYS GOODBYE TO POETRY

my mother's milk turned sour

DE QUIRICO PAINTS THE DISQUIETING MUSES

her milk turned sour because

AND GRAND METAPHYSICAL INTERIOR

Edgar her favourite brother

ARP MAKES HIS

COLLAGE WITH SQUARES ARRANGED ACCORDING TO THE LAWS

OF CHANCE

was killed

AND

ENAK'S TEARS

DOCTOR ZHIVAGO

it's close at the movies
hot as a summer in the Urals
bodies around me peeled from their coats
everyone and no one

"buildings are political"
a girl on my right
she argues her boyfriend disagrees
I make a survey for her instantly
declare the country bankrupt

Zhivago centres the darkness
a puppet face of love and
privilege a poet too
it's hard to believe a poet
on Denman Street and utter silence
not even the crushing of
a candy wrapper

         then to
the cold and the suffering the
iron treasons of Russian life
one side bleeding the
other till someone gives the poet
next time the tyrant
the heavy policeman finally
dropped to his knees

Zhivago and nobody coughs
Zhivago nobody stirs Zhivago
in the terrible wonderful snow-glare
Zhivago liking the ambiance
of his writing table

the broken Zhivago white and queer
in the resurgent city
amongst the lunch pails

the lights go up hands on
my knees I ponder the question
is poetry political heavy moment

out on the street I'm unnerved by
this Twentieth Century
soviet of skyscrapers

in *The Passion of Anna*
Max Von Sydow is the HUMAN ISLAND
we can share his choice but
can he

the cruising camera catches
him treading stiffly off like
a spooked deer in
the snow of his yard

the colour's anemic and long
runnels mark his face for despair
he's brought kindness with
him and books so what

out of island rock
under stationary grey
Evil's loose lynching a beagle
crossing his path with
succuba (once women) the
vessels of love brimming with
love backed-up and stagnant

kisses exchanged seem tender
enough in the gas-white flush or
silhouetted on watery glass
sadness starts to drain

but what alas is turning man
against men Eve against Anna
tugging on steering wheels
slaughtering sheep

raping the flesh
of snow blazing like Fate after
the fire itself has offered
its own capitulation

THE ELEPHANT CELEBES
for Max Ernst

hope has lost a friend
as spaceman's engine failing falls
in yaws of kerosene-black smoke
a celebrant's descent a
dreamer's near catastrophe

a huge inflation called the
Celebes leans against the afternoon
sky between its legs
vacuum hose for sigh and
one that plots its path
a headless nude for docking

metals ride the high
encampment of its back squatters
knife-voiced warriors through sunblack

canister with two-step in its flange
a puff of boiler air
its name implodes
and leaves a mooring mast
a stripped caduceus
to sing to

AFTER HEARING FRANK SCOTT'S TV PLAY
ON THE RONCARELLI CASE
(A Poem For The Roma Restaurant)

it's shameful but
I remember a different place
another crusade

we were campaigners too
whether drinking or swaying painfully
gratefully at the urinals

as that's where it begins
we could start with the food
ravioli — soapy sachets of pasta

spaghetti — white ceramic hemispheres
mysterious alive Chianti my
introduction to an old art

I met Emma Goldman there
(a booth against the wall)
and as counterpoise my cousins

Andrew the one who sang the one
who raged inside the one who had
gifts and wisdom and who died

the one who dropped like moonrock
into Lake St. Louis then
surfaced flat in the morgue without

a cause and mourners minus one

A spiel of grace, an early sunprick for the imagined river;
so it begins as it begins for all the others; long-drawn sound of traffic,
milk bomb at the door, woman coughing uphaa uphaa uphaa.

Barring the way the moss-red brick of Care, grocery window through
which you silently crash swimming into the blood, morning
                                        hallucination
at which I have stared dumbfounded by its opacity.

Once you started to read the "sickness" disappeared. Light from
                              the floor
became attentive. The bed stopped ingesting you through its labial
                              tissues
In fish-bright plane the courier sang. Rimbaud, Artaud,
                              assembled at poem's weightless plunge
The poem slowly withdrawn as if the Underground, your Love, had
                              threatened a burning.

Perhaps I exaggerate, perhaps I was thrown at finding
                              so unexpectedly, so perfectly
a brother so terribly open like a wound. The courier, your
                              pimp-dead girl,
lost in physical blue her half-breasts plastered noons,
                              her mouth of lights unyielding
like a thousand bloodied trilliums.

Jerry Rodolitz with sickness-spaniel hair, six containers of
                              pills by unmade bed,
I want your recipe for incense, your Ginsberg-goddess landed,
I want your twenty-seven years in which you are dying live and
                              unchanging.

Day Off

my day of rest today
                    I need more sleep
                                    no words

TATTOOS
                  Fine Original Designs by
                            Doc Haggis

no sign-collecting
                      no taking of notes
                                that old

lumbercamp cook again
                      I run into him at
                                all times of

the day
            and everywhere
                        (discussed Melville was it

or Pound)
            don't think why
                      what he does in

that bank is probably
                      a wordless transaction
                                      a little

crazy perhaps
                high bloodpressure
                              so far so good

bank pictures who say
                  what's to be hung
                              a Winslow Homer

BREEZING UP
                    children sailing round hats
                                              knee britches

AMERICUNS
                    a sky that's seriously
                                        beautiful

Gaugin a travel
                    picture of Tahiti before
                                        travel pictures

Cezanne mostly water
                         long plane of the water
                                              telescoped

by blue
            the dynamics of the shore
                                  L'Estaque as it

actually is

MELVIN'S HAT

I was writing it Melvin
when Sylvia mentioned your hat
and it became the poem
remember Melvin's hat she asked
and down it dropped like a lemon into the slot
women have this awesome talent for instruction

remember Melvin's hat sure I remember Melvin's hat
and I remember his mind and man's condition in the fifties
I remember Melvin's double-breasted suits
Melvin's shoes — I know — forever black
Melvin's girls Melvin's steady warmth Melvin's cross. . .

Iike some of those attitudes of yours you
wore it too much and certainly wore it too long
the sweat stains on the outside band
(it's not me who's complaining it's her
she says her father hid it at our wedding reception)
instruction again and thoughtless propaganda

but joking aside and as it's sucking the blood
of that earlier poem
I suggest you get someone else to write. . .
mythologize the thing

BIARRITZ

Basque-land oil sculpture of the barricades your flatness reminds me of
                    the discovery of a remarkable cactus extract
the pitch of the dream excursion Beaune Beaune. . .
our coming through coastal woods reactivates the signs coming by car
        ripping like cloth through gypsy relevance (a mockery that might
                            be understood a century from now)
I ask for the time and
when you say the casino is time the answer is right
when I ask you for the season you say the seasons have stopped and I
think of your name like the lustre and peppery bubbles of a fine
                                                    champagne
anchored together with scarlet bolts the houses exhale the streets
                        sleep whiter than novels
we walk the beach and by noon our voices have swerved through the
        lost sand- drawings of Picasso the scandals that rocked a Republic
                        and in which everyone played a role
and by dusk my shirts are all come back bluer than a seaward mile filled
                        with freshness like mother's bodice
I ask you to light the candles (the biggest of all the rose-swirl)
to lay out the gears for another day
and the coupon books

looked out the wlndow played our game
what does he do
pomaded hair the white Cadillac convertible
it was almost too easy and
you were right
a gangster you said

one still night there were
tight pants out on the street
someone being kicked between Lincolns
the gangster's door was
lit like a laundry chute
call the police you said now
wait said I gangsterland is separate

he had sons and a wife the wife
was a French Canadian comely and human
what does she do
rides herd on his call-girls
it wasn't a guess

his sons were like all sons but with
looser style something extra and expendable
what will they do we shook our heads

the gangster died pushed
downstairs on a Chrlstmas Eve — in Bordeaux jail
sinister a full investigation they cried
nothing further was heard

what do they do

ADDICTION

I'm addicted to your body smells
I hope this isn't trivial or unpoetic
(I'd be the first to admit that 'smells' a
heavy word with some raw associations so
I'll try to make a list before
the love bursts out) — the smell of
your hands is a deep-burn version of their touch
today they smell of spices and warmth
the smell of your feet is a vegetable smell like carrots
you could say that feet have country and class
your stomach is the moon culture
your breasts the permanence of dreams
your private parts — the reddish of coleus   the
texture of taro leaves of prickly rhubarb
gunners parting in the tropics
your knees are menthol promontories of desire —
peppermint camphor   sweetness on the freezing spheres of time
your smells in the morning when you're half asleep —
your lips your hair the sheets your breath — some
richly confused collection that's been covered and aged
some charged and arched confection
that brings me to this

THE CANADA KICK

my wife is on a Canada Kick
which means she reads Maclean's
from eleven to twelve a.m.
and meanwhile her Canada is
clogging the drain with some
huge indifference coating the
vertical drop with a fatty substance
half corpu   half blot

and a friend arrives from Montreal
hands me a study he's made of
the Seigniory Club that used to
belong to Louis-Joseph Papineau who
was exiled if you remember   but who
loved this land (the Laurentian Shield)
although it couldn't be farmed
                              and
a footnote said that a certain
Philomon Wright (quick from the USA)
had learned to farm its trees
in nearby Hull 1801

is this where we went wrong
                              and
Queen Victoria coming along like
a massive Buddha on wheels

they say 'till
I half believe it myself
that labour leaders are doing us in
the ones from the "Old Country"
English and Scotch who'd felt an
empire grow and collapse on their backs
"hot line" cranks spewing their brutal
hatred from the underground
of a remembered sub-aristocracy

we who had nursed at those ample
breasts like perpetual children find
what we had to know —
the "lady's" guts were of coal
and caste and foreign submission...

of dust we imported like gold
that drifted — is drifting — across
the eyes of a landscape
unparellaled and yearning

Section Seven

JOHN ABBOTT PLUMBER

at 8 a.m. hits the bell so it sticks
and already talking it up
admits himself   his
sling of tools and his light
and how's the pretty wife

every year   over Sylvia's dead body
super-Blackpool image   yachtsman's cap
the same dun overalls only dirtier
meets her sly complaints with
bug-eyed patronizing
oversolicitousness   the subject
of sex is a constant threat

chancey yes   but he's also my visiting expert
on pre-war English vaudeville types
minor movie stars and folksy entertainers

me   I've been waiting to ask
remember Lynn and Walls?

stopping his work and heavy incomprehension *who?*
silence then rising belligerent question

you mean Tom Walls!

me   I guess so yes

Tom Walls (he's started) *was born on the Fifth of April...*

how's that for plumbing
how's that for service

FOR MARION FULLER WHOSE BIRTHDAY IS
ON THE SAME DAY AS MINE

sister I knew you at once
recognized the profile (a French kid
after briefly sizing me up
"*bonjour Monsieur Rat*")

what you have there is
more like a Renaissance nose
bevelled straight bridge and
forehead in line a little too strong

in a narrow face to be "classic"
(Leonardo used it for angels but
only from the side)

         Picasso — well
surely it's you (a fractious
black-haired version)
centering *Les Demoiselles d'Avignon*
and then there's Nefertiti...

as you probably know
nose is important and even prophetic
(in Japanese a pictograph for
"self" or "private" or Big Nose
their caricature for WASP)

imbalance of nose like imbalance of
love or ambition is a knife of
malingering hungers
the sign of our April birth
incestuous sun white under black

eclipsed by its own potential

GENOA REVISITED 1972

I come hustling on the scene
in my rented Seat having
driven all the way from Madrid
some sort of poetIc encounter seems inevitable
but the way I feel today I've said it all
by living in Montreal Toronto Vancouver
the coast line was beautiful so that's enough
this place has grown as it did
a city with troubles like the others

making like "Bicycle Thief"
I've picked the rim behind the sea a barrier
of sheds a corridor of my non-intentions
I make mistakes get straightened away
in the heavy evening traffic — grazing busses
one eye up to the iron Juliet balconies
the high-stage windows stuffed with the message
some combination of commerce water
power corruption and human style

the cars ride up and there's the Raffeallo
ocean bird last of the liners basket funnels
like basket masts on the Texas
(US battleship rusting away in a Houston park
in case you're curious)
boats are not a digression in Genoa
time perhaps is the one unpardonable flashback
poetry like this is a senseless kind of spin-off

chinks developing between the buildings
houses patches of sea south is obviously the
escape route at the end of
the bus lines clusters of people slow me —
scattering to their non-suburbia at ten o'clock
I should be bedded down in Rapallo
thinking of nothing harder than the looming darkness
not even Ezra Pound

Two Days in Montreal, 1979

I.

did the roots trip
(not like me) windows staring
like familiars on the
sure rich day of my childhood
houses   buildings in
a line close as distant parents
echoing   foreclosing
redolent as blue

> not a hair out of place   not
> a scratch in the mortar of
> home sweet home

and the church still there
and Simpson Street (named I suppose
for the Little Emperor)
Summerhill — named after all I believed
in then as a future poet-eudemoniac
the flower bed   the
signatures of iron
stairs like human gestures —
No. 12 my circus slide
my sisal-coated tongue of "out"
my concertine-ed drawbridge

> and colour in the vaults — winter with
> its mountains and its faults
> knife flash in our cries

II
GUY AT STE. CATHERINE STREET

started down at Liggett's Drugs where the
   girls of Trafalgar School were not allowed to go
where I once sat between the "baby ballerinas" Toumanova
         and Baronova
  slowly losing my life they were stars if I ever saw stars

opposite above the pilasters of the Bank of Commerce Bldg. —
   beside a dentist's office — was the site of my first true studio
painting into Art— a process that grew to the low moans
   of anesthetized patients pictures piling up prying me open
layng me out as a tender mosaic forest

   and the heat hummed French and
   the night spoke French
   and the evening settling into
   the colours of smoke ad exhaustion
   the streetcar driver spoke (silent) French
   the conductor French from his stagey podium of cold
   Branchaud the barber praised and fixed in
   the dead aristocracy of his mirrors
     and mirrored across the way
   the girls at the top of the stairs who
   touched their clients "goodbuy" with
   country affection...

   the Mountain spreading its
   arms of iron and lightbulbs spoke French
   delivery boys a body French of
   thrift and contempt

   and then His (Absent)
Majesty's Theatre —modest face of inside out
Harry Lauder — what was he all about? could this be
grandpa's humour?
black with heart tall with rage — Robeson as Othello
English movies— stilted romance of Imperial burden
hilarious Lynn and Walls (the butler called Death)   laughter
cooked in a skin-tight shroud of tradition and form (totally
alien world) moving our unform lips
breaking us up

years to the night a come-up-ance
my name (understood) in
the credits of Wedding in White
I felt sick

III
ON THE CHILD'S-EYE VIEW

to be heartless — time and
place are melded now   defused
shining like a scrap of flypaper
memory is not the core
this slowly climbing street
was a chrysalis a cell with
cosmic and affectionate components —
a factory wall — wise and flat as weaving
a plaster wedge in finely breeding sky —
the unloved "Medical Arts"
that dead-end street stillborn as
it was 50 years ago   THE CLEANERS
the schoolyard fence — flapping scarf
frozen in the downdraft of
Cote des Neiges
tenements behind the elegant
facade called "Grosvenor"
anything might happen   anything
could happen   nothing did

                      in fact a space apart a space unclaimed
an actionless springboard   a proving ground raised
on a midden of corn husks thighbones and beaver hats

on a match factory and a lumber yard   swell of dry-hued textiles
on staid servility   chronic purity
aborted revolt rising out of the pavement like withered grass

on freedom from a past
on freedom declined by a chinless war
        (fighting — the holiest cult   oldest and sickest profession)
on freedom defined as future debt

a festival space with "festival" a word proscribed
a magic circle planed by ringing light
grooved and shone by squaters

IV
LOOKING BACK AT LINCOLN AVENUE

In the sense of being used from
the truant pool of being called
my days ran out like a wavering fuse
walls were the limits of words
and sawed — off streets
the sudden horizons

brick was the mirroring landscape
(dry red fog of mysteries)
sweetened by seasons of painless light
processed by fine-grained taste flat in
the strirrups of stillness

"main street" now a homeless name
stinking of gin slouching criss-cross into
the paths of hissing machines
the "school house" edged like a social sin
to the rims of this ghetto of wealth

where should I begin

talking   looking into your face
it's hard to believe all that violence
these tortures are dominant
features in our lives
hand prints   necessary cautions

because I'm never aware
of social desperations
or pain in
face to face exchanges
the modest and tenuous
one-eyed connection of sitting
beside you here
the beautiful balancing act of
banging in intimate vocal range   the
sensuous strike   weightless barage
of words
behind my eyes

authority has its distances
pronouncements their official levels
murder its practical hoods and
war its earsplitting silence

it's a perfect day to fumble guileless students into storm troopers
to order the howling girls to cook their fate rather than proclaim it
it's the perfect light to drag some foreign military hornets from their
      faraway hives
to plant them here and there so Allah feels their sting
so Allah blacked by a shameless sun can suck their childish venom
it's a perfect day to raise the temple with growling bisquits from an
      old man's beard
to trap the falling leaf   burn its skin and stem as a hundred thousand
      fists choke in the air
a perfect day to wrap the faceless bloom of life   seize the moons of
      Art as if a gift had been made
a low prostration one more time to man's indulgent myth —
his gilded vice   phoney hairy voice cracking laws like eggs
      chattering in blood

HE

he is beautiful
favours the oldest themes
when posing him questions
riddles he loves laughter splits
the barrel of his might
oh wonderful
he loves to kill

comfort he loves
sympathy and service women
he created for these pressing needs

and here are the words that
brought islands and cities
armadas into play
like so many marbles

children too

the second day of life
he shoulders cloth the third
day of life he scoops a frog
from the frozen pond
the fourth day he renders into law
the great invariables
the fifth day his voice of vaseline and coal is
purged of the three sins   the sixth day
he plasters his face and tragedy is born
and out of tragedy that
fetid ton of laughs that is
his greatest ally in murder
the seventh day is unforgettable
like a cold white log
he rests and farts and formulates
in an almost unnatural way

G U N L O V E G U
N L O V E   for e.e.cummings

and should i unstring
this thung
        AM-AIR-REE-CA
    and
did i never sight
on INjuns while
    sitting on the
OHNO?

Metro*Goldwyn*Millions with
its monster arms
                    and
    strips around
 the globe
& cans & properties...

would i have spatat
Bufflo Bill
            beardafloating
willowthin andtall
                    or
  ANNIOKLEY
steadying her buckskins to keeee-RAK

suffer little children
little Custers
    i could
                sure-you-say
    but what would i
_____
replace
itwith

LEAVING BLOWHOLE BAY   JULY 1977
(*a trip down Tahsis Inlet on the Uchuck Three*)

the sky locked down
like the metal lid of a pressure cooker
turning the steep fjord
into a jungle estuary
an Amazon

an iron boat nosing casually
into the wharves and float camps
strung along the way
the derrick man —
a four-armed Shiva ln
a laundered T-shirt

what is the "revolution" of today?
the pay check surely
what are the sights and sounds
the environments of these
surface mines for trees?
the "cat" banging masticating its movements
the suffocating plugs of
seventh gear a circle of flies
sniffing the stubble of tree stumps
an exposé of light at the lip
of the levelled cut — reluctant
almost yellowish
the grappler lurching — tensing its
single massive arm...

the boom boat rolling grotesquely

adults children
(six or more) approach the gangplank
straggling raw as if
they'd just reshaped from
the crust-coloured rubble
just stepped out of bed
well-loved dogs yawning wagging
their tails peeing on scattered
pieces of luggage

a seaplane grazes our heads and disappears
(poised predacious floats
ominous bird-like pass) its headlight
oozing like the plague

boring smoothly down an
untapped corridor of dampness
narrow cabin cupboard warmth
varnished booths like
a country cafe across the aisle
a pair from Amsterdam eager to
talk logger children brushing by
flushing the narrow spaces
ignorant of city ways
a mother — married woman routing
some desperation through
solitaire...

lists again
sense perceptions as a lifetime craze

reality at either end
no synthesist my mlnd
resists the smothering grip of
modern theologies Marxist or otherwise
do I exist as rooted plant or
is this occupation?
people persist art persists
my cop-out or my *raison d'etre*

the ticket boy and maitre'd
has looseness — ease he grew up
with the boat would
that explain it?
I say that boats are
clearer in my mind than poems
he recommends the homemade soup
(note — fiction
that his hair was grey)

the counter's narrow food OK
a moon of light above us three
a lewd disreputable red

LILLOOET IN JANUARY

I'd almost forgotten land could freeze
that the sun could hibernate like a melon under
ground as hard and cold as a dead man's chin

all connections alive Lillooet is still a village
a road that snakes along like fallen wire separate
buildlngs thin as showcard markers on the
swollen scoop — lull between mountains

its history starts as a starting block for miners
filing in on wooden rails things have settled down
some glossy cars a cruising truck the after-hockey
crowd in the long cafe and licensed lounge facing

the station racial mix that doesn't mix
Hindus are stinking proof that niggers fuck skunks
is writ in semi-script to the right of the toilet
anonymous bait for shivering liberals quietly
doubling back to a "civilized" Vancouver

I was lucky to meet the rodeo king Stanley Alec
(who says he always drank with care) at the
door of the liquor store where else lucky to
catch that red-haired girl sighting her shot
cracking a pair of billiard balls like sexual lightning

tires screech "...garbage!" someone yells at a
fur-clad tourist it's Saturday it's Clowning Day
with just a hint of softness circling the
bucking steer the macho pistons kick setting
slyly round the beehive's blistered hide its
roaring drunken tongue

TRAVELLING VIA RAIL — 3 POEMS

I LEAVING THE LAST TRAIN STOP BEFORE EDMONTON

spare and blond
fiftyish perhaps
exuberant survivor

Ken my husband in an
Edmonton hospital she says
it seems already minus a leg
he fell and broke its stump
in several places
                  nothing I can say

worked still works for the CNR
but here we have our farm we
could never live in town
we've always loved the country
                  nothing I can say

lake and vine of smoke
distant concrete to our right
she turns to talk of oil
gas peat moss coal
massive shovels (English made)
fishing through the ice
                  nothing I can add

workers over there she points
are zipped to job — it seems
against their will — by helicopter —
they just don't seem to like it
                  nothing I can say

heating here? I've always loved it warm
I like to keep my house at
72 degrees she smiles
                  nothing I can say

it's hard to take but
Canada still equates — will always
it seems equate — with "region"
only in the island state of English Montreal did
something rise above those racked preoccupations
dictated to by landscape isolation
(Mediterranean feel said poet Mike Doyle)

North Ontario — god!
turtle shells of granite broken walls of trees
endless lakes suggestlng giant shell holes in
a flooded battlefield
                    ARMSTRONG!
                              and by
coincidence I'm talking Art with a
man from Ohio I tell him excitedly
this place is special...Norval Morrisseau
Indian painter...Woodland School...

he isn't impressed

apart from the station the townsite seems to
end before it begins someone walks away from the
last wood house into the brush ignoring the train

there should be a billboard —
sensual colour rich as rebellious glass
a figure with caliper lips saying (in several tongues)
Norval Morrisseau lived here Benjamin Chee Chee died
for this argosy up from time and place
this foreign travelling of the spirit

Or course I've got it wrong
          (you ought to see his face)
the founding place the citadel is Beardmore not Armstrong
a caliper of road away around Lake Nipigon
and one more name to come — Carl Ray
gothic wlndow mythic sun warped
and coiled in the tidepull blue
the breakers of a single day

III   OLD FRENCH CANADIAN MINER AND WIFE FROM ABITIBI

spare
small red-round eyes behlnd glasses
nasal fin for nose
does language shape the face?

                 dressed expressly for travel
                 hat for lunch
narrow brim (sporty? tight?) fedora type that
I associate with garment makers
Jewish Montreal the "forties"

how old do you think he is? asks
his wife — smiling eager coaxing
four eyes on my face

how old is the string of a fiddle
the gut of work sustained and entertained
for fifteen generations

DRIVING TO SEATTLE

radio and
Rachmaninoff's rasa
(concerto no.2) in
that worn and
unexceptional landscape
stretching south
from Blaine
rasa planted in my
chest (my throat?) like
clotted tangled wool
spilling from the topped
tumblers of my eyes
that I steady
almost in pain
pleasure is uncaring
is indulgence or the
icon of Delight —
a human sun-cum-numen...
you have cross-bred
religions my friend
Serge
we lunched together
once
ate ice cream
50 paired wlth 5
your presence then
(your talk about my spoon)
is still a shadow
plumped with Being
stretched in caring
rasa now
and clip of
worn nostalgia passing
like music

Lemoine Fitzgerald

energy is sometimes
less than a delicate man's
intensity

Barlow's Garage
Doc Snyder's House
poplar trunks like tubers cooked
in winter clarity
              porch and snow
reface the thin close paste of
stucco that is
surface yard   and light measured
to the inch

the artist's eye is
fashioned to the yardstick of
his feeling
crisp
unblinking
and imperative

Bonnard
was born at
Fontenay-aux-Roses in
eighteen sixty-seven
Cézanne's eyes shivered at
the landscape's
suggestion
of dyn-
amics

L'ESTAQUE   L'ESTAQUE

those of us
who constantly
grow old
may wonder
what

happens

SPECIALIST

I feel guilty when
I find you making bread
or when your hands being carefully kissed
smell faintly of spices

placing one of your palms (warm
from sleep) on my face
I ask it if you are for food first
and art second or as it would be with me
food second and art first
(the specialist lying about his priorities
as you might lie about your age

feel this dough you say
read me your latest poem
the terror is that both are in you when
you paint make love with me or
listen while I read unclearly
anguished with doubt

SECHELT

I know it was all my choice but
I'm glad to get the mountains off my back for a while
granite sometimes reminds me of
dead whale hide it tends toward black
and I'm a child of Impressionism
really that was my religion
colour invading shade colour replacing light
the symbolism is clear
anyway here I am
                    out on a sandbar
a happy shipwreck man
an oar set up in the sun to dry
a vertical crack
on the bulging dish   of   the   Strait

her furniture is now on
the wrong side of colour
her house (their house) a bit of pioneering
with wit and style thrown in her shoreline
trees a fan she can raise to deflect the
animal immensity of the lake

a beaver is building a dam on her personal stream
has plastered it lovingly with a
lifeless black alluvium — upholstery again
no one seems able to catch it

she's Swiss she does stitchery   or did —
a postage stamp of Haile Selassie
inch-high Indians Mexican and Red Tahitian
hillsides unhinged by hints of her touching
the vertigo of her miniatured passions

there are time-stalled art magazines about
Swiss with a bias for the Primitives and
the odd abstraction

her husband (much older) treated her like a princess
did all the cooking padded the deal to
include his closest bachelor friend
(*Jules et Jim   ménage a trois*   that was pure romance)
swept her away on the carpets of
his youthful incurable tripping

adjacent (rotting with apples) the orchard has
long since been sold detached from her like
sweet mobility surplus vigour driving sex

like earth from the beads of her
polished ease her living dream

some are born level
to the light native to
the mix so that there
is no fix of
patronization no
throne of sympathy or
blindfold of
disgust no Indians
no foreigners
no poisonous alienation
no God monopolizing love
no Love monopolizing God

love of Being Life
love of
work and leisure

was she one of a kind did the mountains
          incite enchant
the mountains juggle their peaks in the chapters
          of her high decisive ride

was the lake (Okanagan) the kind of
          music women crave
fluid speechless breathless as a lover's weight
                              liquid with surface passions
                              burning with costume flowers
shaping not shaped by the nervous land?
Ceylon's Colombo first to upper class in
stiffly ordered England she
stressed to a friend
what I want is a wild free life!
and then after fourteen children and
living the chances she took the dramas the
open unnamed isolate places
we'd have to agree in
a special sense
she achieved it

it would be hard to imagine
Indians dying of the grippe
but sometimes they did
helplessly twos and threes
                          naturally
                          in drops
                          as
rain soaks into the land
as chaff blows into the sun

we've had slightly more than a hundred years for verification
            infiltration
we've had slightly more than a hundred summers to colour the
            lake-strip Okanagan Blue flood it through our veins pull
            it round the headlands like a liquid sash

we wake to find the black blindfold of the
mountains has been lifted from our eyes
a mountain that remains   has settled itself
rolled on its back glows at the sky like
polished hide a greenish-brown ceramic

            there were of course spectators
            before we came — rye grass high
            as a horseman's shoulder
            ponderosas hesitating looking
            back from the root of a
            vertical track — their
            individual shadows
            Indians who moved in
            lines in packs like
            other animals who
            dreamed of yawning size —
            the unformed God — a death of
            consciousness for all
            they knew...
            Bravery (The Killing Game)
            was rising to this myth —
            Quinisco quite alone
            tracking the grizzly

crowding it at bay stabbing
as the giant hugged
in disbelief

we're not so far away Claude wasn't it me who sold you
that immaculate gun they say that Frenchmen are humano—
centric   they say Canadians (ask Robert Graves) are
natural soldiers clued to the business of killing
sans myth sans motive...
                    and also not so close
Father Pandosy stubborn man of peace heavenly *cultivateur*
and Susan Allison on the Peachland side of the lake —
coyotes (taking the strychnine bait) sometimes vomited and
then ran on as well as ever...often thought how
beastly how cruel we were
        have learned to love
        feel differently

        we   were   so   few

I.

close-hold locked in a
curve-topped space
(propellor blurred out of sight)
a brain before me sliced in half
pulse-clocks prospects nerve-ends
tensions nodules signals signs
Acrobatic Maneuvers Are Limited To The Following:
                              spins and stalls
                              lazy eights
                              chandelles . . .

chased by a pair of wings
the world starts dropping its wonders below
like a flustered criminal
houses look up from their private ring of trees
like uncut cedar eyes
chants Claude to a locked-in ear —
      this is Sierra Alpha Juliette
            this is Sierra Alpha Juliette
still flylng low but
flying as high as Canadians
ever fly wlth words

distanced powdered by height
the City dismissed
shuddering slithering space—inches up
the Texada side of the Strait
islands below are evergreen pelts
laid out to dry on the dense
blue tile of the water
shoreline a rising rug of trees
novel soaked in the vowel "U"
endless grumble of "U" soaked prose

II.

times are checked route aligned
sharp-blurred profile as Claude on
an empty coin of light —
Emperor of Views Gallic muse of Tech.
Gifted half-son of what could
still be a life-loving Science
(but like this air Plenty all about us yet
so no objections no defections)
we speak in pointings smiles
legs tucked up exhilaratlon cupped in
a silver cobweb of space
in lift and risk of flight I ask myself
       just how many times do I swallow
           say in a minute
how fast is my heartbeat

the top of the Strait
solid cluster of islands
jigsaw chips of a moss-rotting puzzle
we swerve and bank
our eyes spill blackly down on
an endless coastal script
somewhere below a friend has a hideout
"somewhere" curves out "somewhere" cuts in
nowhere says here

III.   REDONDA EAST REDONDA WEST HISTORIES ETC.
         NAMES ABOUT LIKE AGING VERBAL STAINS

Discovery Passage proof of split and
corridor of dangers
Discovery was a "His Majesty's" ship

    Heriot Bay whose boats
    were launched with ceremony —
    maidens in flowing white reciting poetry
    as water met with fashioned wood

Cape Mudge where then espousing 'white'
Chieftain Billy Assu orders his longhouse etcetera
pushed over the cliff

Cortes — colour of heat and fist—wipe of power
Whaletown — short lived wail of slaughter
whalevoid now

Read Quadra gentleman Vancouver claimed and
officer from Spain whose name was graded back
erased because of Imperial failure

loggers sober loggers skilled loggers crushed
loggers drunk and craziest...but wait
an integrated school

treacherous pool whipped into twenty foot
curl of knives by southeast wind
fishermens' ghosts and cries curses   and   sweat
purdahs spits   and   whirlpools

IV.

Campbell River — this is me
Sierra Alpha Juliette
pointed there distanced from you here...
sharp exact a woman's voice replies
clears us to land clues us in
for Campbell River strip
our nose through cramped and angled glass
leads us round a wide slow turn
then miles of gentle drop
water wedge of suburbs sulk of snow-tipped
peaks pass a corner of the eye
now details flowing by
details turning clear —
scrub and country roads
trees — aspen-fragile tactile dry
fences pole and wire fields...
the moment holds its breath
brutal touch of wheels on tarmac
Claude as equal now relaxed
my senses flooded spirit bright
body feels its weight
says this is home

creating its own
icing-pocked rut-ridden road
the ferry pulls away
we sit about in slanting shade from
funnels faked like
giant yellow tarot cards

Indians grouped here but
only in winter for ceremonies
Kwakiutl Nimpkish
can I sense who they are how they feel
the sun this floating ease the
crust-white curve of fading
Spread Legs Beach is how I'll
sum this up at least for today

but this is Bakoos or was the season
to work together not play and lately
soccer wages whiplash and what...
the preacher in modest informals —
"Miss Carr stayed there"
prim Victorian gables greenish-grey
while up the hill the massive bighouse smile
spreads wider into space with
chanting in its petals

BREAKFAST IN HORSESHOE BAY

a fjord
very last
farthest down the coast
windows breast on light
breakfast in the warm
dark sweaters of wood
what should be good is bad
as women grow more lovely as
I age   their voices —
tactile gems of sound
hands wrists skin hair profiles lips...
slavery I feel
girl to man —
      is this a good place to sit?
      is the sun in your eyes?
waitress (graced with beauties too)
      the paper sir?
uh. . . yes
a muffin like a puffed-up bird
centering my plate
TOP RED DEAD   POSTAL PEACE
clumsy beat of news
so persistent false
but anyway distracting

My Part Of B.C.

I would like to know...but never will
like to have known the slug-tipped pace
the roughness of this land
the not quite ancient black and white of its
perpendicularities —
these and nothing else
lenses no theorems no myths...another time
a reference or two might add but histories curve a
line so short it scares me
40,000 years ago the first pre-Indians —
"Indian" — so faked a name!
Marpole — pretty close but pretty far
the taste of what they ate and not its cradle word
the touch of what they saw
the need for doing what they did the great
green-black enclosures — neither friend nor foe

EDSON, ALBERTA

a desert claimed Simpson defending
his empire and word spread
out like a locust plague

what would he say to Edson
this day before the Rodeo-Stampede
mainstreet —

sign-stacked   garrulous   sunstruck
floating in mud from
last night's rain pipeline —
straight   source in its
self-styled vein
buried at either end

cars like bugs in the feeding posture   trucks as
huge and dusty grey as
buffaloes were dusty black
ranks of tractors shone to
carve the earth with vast
cosmetic grooves and twists

my waitress? —well a cowboy hat of
chocolate felt its curves so
thin and real repeated in her face
boyfriend —tight as work-scuffed rods
props against the counter
spins his love song
through a toothpick

present time
a roadside near Saigon though more like
a rolling tropical England
I ask directions from a sun-baked farmer
who explains (in English)
he wasn't always like this
wielding mattock or pickaxe...

indicates a lime-stained footpath
It's very still and warm
stone fences which land me in
a suburban rooming house or pension
dark high ceilings like I imagine in Bloomsbury
(if I ever imagined Bloomsbury)
someone's standing in my way playing a violin
Ignores me doesn't budge from centre stage
pythistic type a bony Celt a Beardsley
Percy Grainger who I've met before in the
doorway of these old radio studios

I'm back in the lobby of this same
small rooming house-hotel of Southern France-
Galveston-Tangiers-Vera Cruz (actually Saigon)
the proprietess comes out to size me up
she doesn't smile (English again an Angela Lansbury)
you can't stay here she says ungracefully

I feel dismayed a big mistake I say
and you should know I'm editor. . .one of the editors
of *Travel Magazine*

(Grandbois is of course the Editor)

her son and bouncer makes a profile by the door
a tableau of indifference contempt

I'm on the street   weather warm and sultry
a Rue du Bac   and there's a market near
which could be Mexico-Saigon
or just the vibrant constant meeting of
the world's non-poets

first heard the noise
or should I say staccato of words
plates of female sound
bouncing off the lifeless street
      ...AND I FINALLY GOT PAID
      (long pause)
UP THOSE BLOODY STAIRS AND
      THEN I FELL...
      O.K. O.K. IT WASN'T MY FAULT
      (pause)
      LADIES BE NOT OUTSHAMED OF YOUR BEAUTY...

bare arms short hair black slacks
sits on the stairs of the tall-cave
entrance to the Bonair Apts
steep dark throat to broadcast her life
her fractured obsessions

note-pen still in hand
I decide to confront pause by
the tips of her pointing socks
      I know who you are she says
      you're the meterman
      (normal sound)
      no well give me that and
      I'll show you how he looks
she starts to draw on her slacks
stops says sadly
      I'm covered with graphite
are you an artist I ask

      I was...a long time ago

this street of business warehouse and
Bonair Apts stays strangely deserted the
freeway almost above — perpetual shade
the city's distant heights gracing
the line of the roofs
like a concrete bouquet

I move and
she starts up again
(sadly violent starts and stops)
I try to catch sense but I'm much too close
am projected out and away —
vivid slats from her straining throat

TRIP TO SEATTLE   (THE LITTLE CAR)

passing the border
Peace Arch bare as a dinosaur tooth
happily on the go
like claws of shade ln the evergreens
some trace left some space left for
those jets of change and commitment to
nurture or explode I hope

demolish this driving style
which is all too clearly me my past
the artist voice the poet
speed refined removed
never crude or slavish to movement
the blue-grey shine of my car
wiping the gape and audience of trees
toothless flash —
a cleanser you could say

clips of wood-sheathed presence
EXITs slipping by
Bellingham — red and roll of royal sound
the quills of the churches melted
if they stood at all
my religion — languaging the senses
stillness ln the malls of noon
haze on caves of hate and passion —
Cavendish of gangs

lavish Skajit — greens and growth
could I have been a gambler or
a tamer of land
a criminal against the Bands a
settled spike like Marcus and Narcissa *
but why rave on — complain
being more alive inside this
sailing metal cage
this theatre on the go
than any sulking mind

*Dr. Marcus Whitman and his wife Narcissa were the first white settlers in the US Pacific Northwest

horizon line of sea slides out
past both sides of my vision
out in front an island called Stewart —
a gentle soft-edged murmuring
strung along this horizontal and
scratched above its top
a faded script of the Cascades
fish boats stopped or drifting as if
they'd all been discarded
an eagle high up on a tiny branch
weightless — woven into summer's blue
a single word for this is PEACE
Nature's soundless boundless feast
all-composing all-deceiving stillness

MORNING ABOVE PEACHLAND

blinding silver sphere —
the sun just up balancing
on Ogopogo's stone image
strung out on the lake

I'm quite alone and high
enough to shout for joy in silence
my shadow stretches thirty feet behind
along a cranium of slight depressions
stones and ponderosa needles between
some dried out berry shrubs
that could be saskatoons

a matchless fusion where I stand
of passion and tranquillity while
tracking from my feet two
flattened blue-black trouser legs like
poles conceived by carpets
or narrowed ferry smokestacks from
those rough-luck good old days

SALTSPRING ISLAND

first day of spring
we've come to sleep
on the island
believe me it's true at
a place called Vesuvius

across the water
sits Crofton
pencils of smoke
shoot to the sky like
white disintigrating poplars

these and the pulp mill's
language of angles seem
to grow out of the earth
which of course they don't

the only motel a domestic
white inside and out
a couple of flower prints
tending to disappear
a heater that pulses ticks
and implodes through
much of the night

it could have been 5 a.m.
blackness clouding the walls
shadowing me
ruling the space
I felt a sudden urge to merge
dissolve myself for good
into this empty vital
pepper-dark anonimity

RAIN

it's raining individual drops
it's raining the long grey sparks of anxiety
it's raining nights and extinctions and warnings and shelters
it's raining a history called Women's Relief
it's raining the copper forms of skyscrapers and the passions of coffee
        and the menus bursting into cabbage rolls
it's raining in the prints of Hiroshige in the memory of Majas in the
        string-plucked oceans of Iannis Xenakis
it's raining into thickets on the Queen Charlotte Islands
it's raining Chinese proper names into the unpacific Pacific
it's raining Mondays and Tuesdays
it's raining up the city from its secret platforms
it's raining down the Revolution from its perilous marquis on the
        Embarcadero
it's raining the souls of housemaids in unwholesome poems
it's raining games of darkness for the children travelling from A to B
it's raining Europeans who have mastered the rain it's raining Japanese
        who expose themselves like film in its brief kimono
it's raining moss and mindlessness and surrenders
it's raining down the ladders of wasps and the life form of trees and
        the privacy of seeds
it's raining on boxes and roof tops and murders and fountains
it's raining on the trunks of stampeding elephants
it's raining on the Great First Digit buried in the middens of
        Mount Vancouver

CLIMATE

this could be a poem
about cold or death or sensuality
or contradiction
the place is a delicatessen the
month November the principal actor
whatever he wanted to say said
"I'm sixty-seven and I'm going to die"
not die here I thought not in this poem
I was just beginning to handle flint and
the sidewalk   hibernation and window-glass
and what had I gone and said about winter...

      I remember Cape Cod — a beautiful couple
      who'd lived through war and art-fed mystical intelligence
      their car which always stood in attendance
      was a green torpedo-shaped Studebaker sedan
      (twenty thousand miles in fifteen years)
      when I sat on
      the beach with them
      it was Cannes in nineteen twenty-eight...
      "you know (the husband apologetically) we're seventy and
      we can't believe it"

"it's all been nothing pointless"
he continues madly   I look around at
the blood-puffed winter skins   overcoats hanging about
like discarded bladders I bite in my smoked-meat sandwich
SEVEN LAYERS OF MEAT a hefty deposit in
The First Starvation Bank of America...
distract him I thought ask him
where the riot is
I really wanted to blurt that
he'd written a single marvellous poem   he had

I wanted to roll the event in a single word like "climate"

CYCLE

when I was five my smile of innocent pain my smile wider than a
               circle was stretched on a frame of bird bones
when I was nine starched cocoons clamps and couplings heart-race
               frozen on a winter sky
when I was twelve the sun burned everything white except my eyes
when I was seventeen I hung out the aura of women in sixteen
               shades of yellow dye
when I was thirty-five snow fell out of the bookshelves   myth rose
               up as a raspberry coloured billboard
when I was forty-six I mortgaged significant pastures pasted my
               manly pin-up
on ancestral temples blue-baked T-shirt boneless limbs like Shiva
when I was fifty-eight stillness blocked me with its arm of roots
which inflections had shaped the paling like neon fruit?
what cool juice could break the imprint on my face?